C.S. LEWIS AND THE TRUTH OF MYTH

Mark Edwards Freshwater

UNIVERSITY
PRESS OF
AMERICA

Copyright © 1988 by

University Press of America,® Inc.

4720 Boston Way
Lanham, MD 20706

3 Henrietta Street
London WC2E 8LU England

All rights reserved

Printed in the United States of America

British Cataloging in Publication Information Available

Library of Congress Cataloging-in-Publication Data

Freshwater, Mark Edwards, 1948–
C.S. Lewis and the truth of myth / by Mark Edwards Freshwater.
p. cm.
Bibliography: p.
Includes index.
1. Lewis, C.S. (Clive Staples), 1898–1963—Criticism and
Interpretation. 2. Lewis, C.S. (Clive Staples), 1898–1963—
Religion. 3. Christian literature, English—History and criticism.
4. Myth in literature. I. Title. II. Title: C.S. Lewis and the
truth of myth.
PR6023.E926Z647   1988
828'.91209—dc 19   87–31704 CIP
ISBN 0–8191–6784–3 (alk. paper)
ISBN 0–8191–6785–1 (pbk. : alk. paper)

All University Press of America books are produced on acid-free
paper which exceeds the minimum standards set by the National
Historical Publications and Records Commission.

To JOYCE

Proverbs 31:10

ACKNOWLEDGEMENTS

I want to thank Dr. Lawrence Cunningham of FLorida State University for his encouragement, suggestions, and continuing support during the writing of this book. I would also like to thank Dr. Walter Moore, Dr. John Carey, and Dr. Leon Golden for their helpful suggestions and comments.

A special debt of appreciation is owed to my wife Joyce whose caring concern, editorial assistance, and computer expertise made this book possible. Thanks also goes to Houston Farrow of ABAX Data Systems for his willingness to instruct us in the complexities of computer technology.

Finally, a special thanks goes to my parents, Fred and Joanna Freshwater, who always kept the faith, and my in-laws, Roy and Eleanor Ringsmith, who stuck with us through thick and thin in "the summer that was."

TABLE OF CONTENTS

ACKNOWLEDGEMENTS..................................v

INTRODUCTION......................................ix

1. C.S. LEWIS: LIFE, WORKS, INFLUENCES..............1

2. LEWIS'S CONVERSION TO "MYTH BECOME FACT"........27

3. C. S. LEWIS AND NEW TESTAMENT SCHOLARSHIP.......55

    Jesus's Divinity...........................56
    The Kingdom of God.........................63
    The Miraculous.............................68
    The Historical Validity of the Gospels.....71
    Conclusion.................................80

4. CHRIST AND ASLAN................................87

5. THE TRUTH OF MYTH..............................121

BIBLIOGRAPHY.....................................131

INDEX..141

INTRODUCTION

C. S. Lewis was a man of many paradoxes: an atheist become Christian apologist; a literary critic writing theology; a bachelor (for much of his life) defending Christian marriage; and a logician defending the idea of myth. Perhaps part of the lasting appeal of Lewis's work is that these writings approach reality from a variety of perspectives. As Margaret Patterson Hanney was to write in the preface to her book <u>C. S. Lewis</u>: "Lewis emerges as a man haunted by longing, a man both passionately romantic and scrupulously logical, a man who, through love and suffering progressed from dogmatism to gentleness. . . . The logic of his prose masks a visionary core."

Much of this "visionary core" revolved around Lewis's concept of myth as the conveyor of truths which can not be perceived through any other medium. For Lewis a myth was not a story which though once believed has since proved to be false. Instead Lewis discussed what he felt to be the essential nature of myth in his book <u>Miracles</u>: "This involves the belief that Myth in general is not merely misunderstood history (as Euhemerus thought) nor diabolical illusion (as some of the Fathers thought) nor priestly lying (as the philosophers of the Enlightenment thought) but, at its best a real though unfocused gleam of divine truth falling on human imagination."

Lewis's conversion to Christianity involved to a substantial degree his recognition of CHristianity as "myth become fact." Lewis had from his youth been deeply touched by the power of myth. But his gradual discovery that the power of myth was united with the actuality of history was a life-changing event. Lewis fully believed that the stories actually fulfilled in the historical life and death of Jesus of Nazareth. Christianity, while not ceasing to be myth, becomes historical fact.

Lewis's recognition of these mythical aspects of Christianity allowed him to recreate that mythology in a new setting in his children's series <u>The Narnia Chronicles</u>. Lewis was able to create a mythical beast named Aslan who in many ways paralleled the Biblical

Christ but in a different and therefore mind-expanding setting.

It is our purpose to examine not only Lewis's views of Christianity generally but to see in his views of myth a "signal of transcendence," a gleam of the supernatural. This signal points to the reality of Lewis's God-centered world view in a way which goes beyond the arguments about the original documents recording Christianity's beginnings. Lewis has achieved fame in the years since his death as the logical apologist for the Christian faith. However, it may be Lewis's creative retelling of the Christian story in a fictional setting which shows that Christianity is truly "myth become fact."

CHAPTER ONE

C. S. LEWIS: LIFE, WORKS, INFLUENCES

C. S. Lewis is one of the most widely read apologists for the Christian faith in the Twentieth Century. Since his death on November 22, 1963, sales of Lewis's books are at an all time high. Part of Lewis's popularity results from the variety of his interests. His writings cover a number of diverse areas. At various times, Lewis wrote poetry, theology, literary criticism, science fiction, and children's stories.

In the second chapter of his book <u>Bright Shadow of Reality: C. S. Lewis and the Feeling Intellect</u>, Corbin Scott Carnell pointed out that Lewis has at least four separate groups of readers. First, there is the scholarly audience, who sees in his <u>Allegory of Love</u>, <u>Preface to Paradise Lost</u>, and his books on Sixteenth Century English literature some of the best scholarly analysis of recent times. Lewis approached literature creatively, letting the work "speak for itself", while showing a marked impatience for scholarly clichés substituting for thought.

A second group includes the readers of his "lay" theological and philosophical works on the nature of Christianity and morality. Again, Lewis attempted to speak to theological questions without speaking theologically. He rejected religious jargon whenever possible. These works have not only been accepted by the general public but have been well received by a variety of critics, including Paul Holmer, W. H. Auden, Charles Hartshorne, Etienne Gilson, and Gilbert Meilander.

Another following consists of lovers of "fantastic fiction," as seen in Lewis's interplanetary trilogy: <u>Out of the Silent Planet</u>, <u>Perelandra</u>, and <u>That Hideous Strength</u>. These works are written in the style of a Christian H. G. Wells, mingling rocket ships and faraway planets with the doctrines of the fall of man and the second coming.

Finally, Lewis has an increasing audience as a writer of children's stories. The <u>Narnia Chronicles</u>

have been described by Roger Lancelyn Green, an authority on juvenile fiction, as among the best children's literature written in this century. Lewis's final volume in the series, <u>The Last Battle</u>, won the Carnegie Medal for the best children's book published in 1956.

Chad Walsh, a prominent Lewis critic, sees in Lewis's work a writer who is able to combine two sensibilities.[1] One aspect of Lewis's style reflects his logical, analytic approach; stressing the importance of reason, clear arguments in debate, and a refusal to gloss over opposing arguments. This approach is usually developed most fully in his scholarly and apologetic works.

The other aspect of Lewis the writer is the fantasizer, the creator of imagined worlds, the revealer of mankind's most deeply felt emotions. For example, in Lewis's book <u>Till We Have Faces</u>, we are presented with a thorough reworking of the legend of Cupid and Psyche. Rather than attempting to analyze the human personality through reason, Lewis attempted to portray its innermost workings through myth, making the myth come alive through fictional narrative.

However, even in his most analytical work, Lewis retained an imaginative style, and in his most fantastic fiction he maintained a logical, analytic approach. It is the combination of these two aspects that Walsh finds most impressive. According to Lewis, reality can only be understood through both approaches, logic and myth. This is one reason Lewis found Christianity attractive; since it combines both elements, it is "myth become fact."

Lewis was born on November 29, 1898, in County Down of Northern Ireland. Because of the wet weather of Northern Ireland, Clive Lewis and his older brother Warren spent a great deal of time indoors drawing, writing, and reading. Even as a child Lewis was fascinated with myth, legend, folklore, and logic. Lewis's father worked as a solicitor in Belfast and was somewhat moody. Lewis was more comfortable with his mother, who behaved consistently in a cheerful, affectionate way. When his mother died of cancer in 1908, Lewis's life changed dramatically. Lewis's father sent him and his brother to a series of preparatory schools, some good and some quite bad. Although he attended Oxford and published two volumes of poetry in the 1920's, <u>Spirits in Bondage</u> and <u>Dymer</u>, both works met with little critical success. It was not until after Lewis converted to Christianity at the age of 32 that he became a successful writer. Further, although Lewis continued to write verse for the rest of his life, he made no serious effort at additional publication in verse form.

At the age of thirty-five, Lewis published his first book of prose, <u>The Pilgrim's Regress: An Allegorical Apology for Christianity, Reason, and Romanticism</u>. In this book, the use of allegory relates the feelings and beliefs which eventually led to Lewis's conversion. This work was not only a defense of Christianity but also an attack on almost every form of thinking of the time, including socialism, liberalism, fascism, and communism. Even Lewis recognized the shrillness of some of his verbal onslaughts and apologized in a later edition for the harshness of his criticisms. Still, in this first work are found most of the themes that Lewis would develop for the rest of his life.

Up to this point in Lewis's life, he had achieved a modest reputation as a poet and religious writer but had not produced a major work of literary scholarship. Finally, in 1936, Lewis's book <u>The Allegory of Love: A Study in Medieval Tradition</u> was published. It was a literary study that assured him scholarly respect and is still regarded as one of the best examinations ever done of romantic medieval literature. Ironically, the book is often mentioned by those critics who deplore the later diversion of Lewis's energies into religious writing. As one Oxford scholar told Chad Walsh: "If only Lewis had followed up <u>The Allegory</u> with other equally important books in literary history, instead of that other stuff."[2]

The <u>Allegory of Love</u> deals with the evolution of allegory as a literary form from Greco-Roman times to the Elizabethan period. It also deals with the strange history of courtly love, which began in southern France during the early Middle Ages. Lewis traced the gradual process by which the idea of courtly love merges with the concept of marriage. By the time of Spenser's <u>Fairie Queene</u>, the newest novelty is romantic marriage. The literary and cultural elements of the book come together in Lewis's consideration of the ways in which the allegorical form was used to express changing patterns of love.

After the publication of The Allegory of Love, Lewis alternated his works of scholarship with other books on imaginative and religious themes. Out of the Silent Planet, his first science fiction work, was published in 1938. Rehabilitations and Other Essays, a series of writings on literature and education, was published in 1939. In the same year, The Personal Heresy was published, in which Lewis conducted a written debate with E. M. W. Tillyard about the correct theory of poetry.

In 1940, Lewis published his first book dealing with a specific theological difficulty. He entitled it The Problem of Pain. He wrote it at the suggestion of a publisher who was bringing out a "Christian Challenge" series dealing in popular style with aspects of the Christian religion. The work was a success and gave Lewis a large following among "lay" Christians.

Some critics found The Problem of Pain too simplistic. Lewis himself later admitted that the book may have been a little too "pat." He quoted, with evident approval, the comment by Charles Williams that the comforters of Job were "the sort of people who wrote books on the Problem of Pain."[3] Most Lewis critics feel that The Problem of Pain should be read in conjunction with his later book A Grief Observed, published in 1961 after Lewis's wife succumbed to a long and bitter struggle with cancer. Nevertheless, The Problem of Pain deals not only with the specific problem of suffering but also with the nature of the Christian religion itself. The themes in this book were later to be expanded in Lewis's other theological works.

In 1942, Lewis published A Preface to "Paradise Lost", not only an analysis of Milton's work but also a defence of epic poetry as a literary genre. That same year Lewis published The Screwtape Letters, a presentation of Christian ethics as seen from the Devil's point of view. The form Lewis chose was a series of letters from Screwtape, an experienced tempter in the "Infernal Civil Service," to his young nephew Wormwood. Wormwood is trying to undermine the faith of a newly converted Christian and is being instructed by his uncle in the proper strategies. The book, tremendously successful, made Lewis internationally known as a popular defender of the Christian faith. It was not universally applauded, however. Lewis cited the letter of a country clergyman who wrote that "much of the advice given in these letters seemed to him not only erroneous but positively diabolical."[4] It was also one of the most difficult books for Lewis to write: "all dust, grit, thirst, and itch."[5] Still, by combining religious doctrine with creative fantasy, Lewis reached an audience which had not been touched by his strictly theological work.

Partly as a result of his growing fame, Lewis was invited by the British Broadcasting Corporation to give a series of talks on Christianity. He gave a series of four radio talks in 1941, and during the next few years, he delivered several additional talks. A revised version of his various radio lectures was published in three separate volumes: Broadcast Talks (1942), Christian Behavior (1943) and Beyond Personality (1944). Later Lewis revised these books and combined them into one volume: Mere Christianity (1952). Together, the sales of these books rival those of Screwtape and are considered the best summaries of Lewis's own theological beliefs. Lewis continued to publish imaginative fiction during this time, bringing out the last two volumes of his science fiction trilogy: Perelandra (1943) and That Hideous Strength (1945). He also wrote The Great Divorce (1945), a fantasy visit to both heaven and hell which is, not unexpectedly, full of surprises.

Lewis published a more general philosophical work in 1945 entitled The Abolition of Man. Although not a specifically Christian book, it is a sustained attack on all philosophies that attempt to "explain away" the moral sense. Stressing that cultural diversities in ethics have been exaggerated, Lewis speaks of the "Tao," the Way, a common ethical framework underlying all major cultures.

Lewis's next specifically Christian apologetic work was Miracles: A Preliminary Study (1947), which deals with the specific theological problem of the miraculous as found in the New Testament. His approach in this book was sharply criticized in a debate Lewis had with the Catholic philosopher, Elizabeth Anscombe.[6] Lewis brought out a revised edition of <u>Miracles</u> in 1960, rewriting chapter three: "The Cardinal Difficulty with Naturalism."

Interestingly enough, Lewis wrote no further books of Christian apologetics for ten years, apart from a collection of sermons entitled <u>Transposition and Other Addresses</u> (1949). When he did publish another apologetic work, <u>Reflections on the Psalms</u> (1958), it dealt with the theological themes of the Psalms themselves and did not attempt any intellectual proofs of theism and Christianity.

Lewis continued his scholarly writing and in 1954 published volume three of <u>The Oxford History of English Literature</u> (privately nicknamed by Lewis "O'HEL"), entitled <u>English Literature in the Sixteenth Century, Excluding Drama</u>. This book deals with the flowering of English literature in the 1500's, while at the same time criticizing the sharp distinction some scholars have made between the Medieval and Renaissance points of view. In fact, Lewis suspected that "the Renaissance" as popularly understood might be nothing more than a figment of scholarly imagination.

Meanwhile, Lewis's talents as a writer enabled him to enter a new field, children's literature. In 1950, <u>The Lion, the Witch, and the Wardrobe</u> was published and was an instant critical and popular success. At the rate of about one a year, the other <u>Chronicles of Narnia</u> were published for an increasingly appreciative audience: <u>Prince Caspian</u> (1951), <u>The Voyage of the "Dawn Treader"</u> (1952), <u>The Silver Chair</u> (1953), <u>The Horse and His Boy</u> (1954), <u>The Magician's Nephew</u> (1955), and <u>The Last Battle</u> (1956). The first volume, Lewis explained, is an answer to the question "What might Christ be like if there really were a world like Narnia, and He chose to be incarnate and die and rise again in that world as He actually has done in ours?"[7]

Children (or adults) who read the <u>Narnia Chronicles</u> experience many of the important events of the Christian story as they might have happened in another world. But the characters in the stories are not merely allegorical types. The Christian story is reimagined rather than allegorized. The reader is free to interpret the stories as Christian or not, and the characters exist in their own right, not simply as symbols. Aslan, for example, is a Christ figure for Narnia, but he is definitely incarnated as a lion, not merely as a man dressed in a lion's costume.

In 1955, Lewis's long awaited spiritual autobiography appeared: <u>Surprised by Joy: The Shape of My Early Life</u>. Much of Lewis's spiritual pilgrimage is presented here, tracing the parallel movements of his intellectual thought with a more mystical experience of Joy, or as Lewis preferred--<u>Sehnsucht</u> ("longing"). Lewis defined <u>Sehnsucht</u> as an unsatisfied desire which is itself more desirable than any other satisfaction. Unlike other desires, the object of this desire is often unknown or mysterious. Lewis's autobiography is the account of his search for the object of his longing and his discovery, at last, that the longing was for union with God. Lewis described his conversion to Christianity as a gradual, drawn-out process and makes explicit here what was only hinted at or briefly mentioned in his earlier apologetic books.

In 1954, Lewis became a Professor--not at Oxford, where he had served as a fellow and tutor since the 1920's--but at Cambridge. Cambridge had invited Lewis to accept a new "Professorship of Medieval and Renaissance English." In his inaugural address, Lewis referred to himself as a dinosaur or "Old Western Man." He told the audience that the "great divide" was not between the Middle Ages and the Renaissance but somewhere between the early Nineteenth Century and the present. For Lewis, the divide was the Industrial Revolution. This separated what Lewis called "Old Western Culture" from the "post-Christian" mechanical society of the present day.

Lewis further argued that paganism and Christianity shared more in common than either shared with a secularized modern world. Lewis concluded that his intellectual roots remained in the previous age: "I read as a native texts that you must read as foreigners. . . . Where I fail as a critic, I may yet be useful as a specimen. I would even dare to go further. Speaking not only for myself but for all other Old Western men whom you may meet, I would say, use your specimens while you can. There are not going to be many more dinosaurs."[8]

At this time, Lewis had become friends by mail with the American author, Joy Davidman Gresham, who had become a Christian in her thirties, largely through the influence of Lewis's writings. After her divorce from her first husband, William Lindsay Gresham, she and her two sons moved to Headington, England, to be Lewis's neighbors. As Lewis and Ms. Davidman became more involved with each other, the British Home Office, giving no reason, refused to renew Ms. Davidman's residence permit. Lewis then, on April 23, 1956, married Ms. Davidman at the Oxford registry office. Lewis at this point claimed to view their marriage as a "legal fiction," a means of giving Ms. Davidman and her two boys British nationality. However, when it was discovered that Lewis's "wife" was dying of cancer, Lewis married her again. This time it was a religious ceremony performed at her bedside in a hospital in the spring of 1957. Only then did Lewis consider himself truly married.

Remarkably, a temporary remission of the cancer occurred, and Joy and "Jack" Lewis had three extremely happy years together. During this time they traveled to Greece together. This was Lewis's first visit to the Continent since his service in World War I.

While married to Joy, Lewis published several books. One of these, <u>Till We Have Faces</u> (1956), is a reworking of the Psyche and Cupid myth, told in the first person from a woman's point of view. Some critics have detected in Lewis's earlier works an undercurrent of "sexism," and Lewis's marriage may have helped him overcome this tendency.

Lewis also published his first specifically apologetic work since <u>Miracles</u> and his first detailed examination of Biblical texts: <u>Reflections on the Psalms</u> (1958). He did another series of radio talks on the four types of human love and how they reflect or relate to Divine Love. This was published in book form as <u>The Four Loves</u> in 1960. Again, most critics feel his insights into male-female relationships in <u>The Four Loves</u> surpass anything on the subject in his earlier writings when he was a "confirmed" bachelor.

Joy's cancer returned, however, and she died on

July 13, 1960. According to Chad Walsh, an American critic and personal acquaintance of Lewis, Lewis never really recovered from this blow. Lewis's own health began to fail, and he suffered from a combination of heart and kidney ailments.

Lewis continued to write, publishing <u>A Grief Observed</u> (1961), a fictionalized account of his own bereavement after his wife's death. Lewis, at first, published the work under a pseudonym, N. W. Clerk, perhaps because of the narrator's bitter questioning of the Divine Will after his grievous loss. Ironically, before Lewis's authorship of the book became public, several of his friends sent him copies of the book, hoping it would help Lewis deal with his own sense of hurt and loss. Perhaps Lewis's writing of the book actually did.

Several books were published in the last three years of Lewis's life and several more posthumously. <u>Studies in Words</u> (1960) is again a scholarly work, an analysis of seven words, their origins and varieties of meanings: nature, sad, wit, free, sense, simple and conscience. This work is not only an exercise in linguistics but also an illustration of the effects that changing cultural patterns have on language.

<u>The World's Last Night and Other Essays</u> (1960) is a collection of essays (most previously published elsewhere) dealing with Christianity and ethical values. <u>An Experiment in Criticism</u> (1961) was an exploration of the subject of literary criticism approached from the reader's point of view. According to Lewis, in good reading we should be concerned less in altering our own opinions than in entering fully into the opinions of others. As Lewis puts it: "In reading great literature I become a thousand men and yet remain myself."[9]

The last strictly apologetic book Lewis was to write is <u>Letters to Malcolm: Chiefly on Prayer</u>, published posthumously in 1964. This book is written in the informal style of "letters," or responses to a fictitious Christian friend. The letters touch on a variety of subjects, including types of prayer, the difficulties of the Christian life, and modern Biblical scholarship. They are a final summary of Lewis's theological views.

Lewis died on November 22, 1963, and several other books have been published posthumously. These include The Discarded Image (1964), a summary of the medieval world-view; Studies in Medieval and Renaissance Literature (1966), a series of scholarly essays; Christian Reflections (1967), a collection of journalistic essays on the Christian faith, Spenser's Images of Life (1967); Selected Literary Essays (1969), writings dealing with English literature; God in the Dock (1970), more essays on religion; and On Stories (1982), a series of non-scholarly essays on fantasy and science fiction. The most recent posthumous work is Present Concerns (1986), a collection of newspaper articles by Lewis on a variety of subjects.

Though his published works were written over a period of thirty years, there is a remarkable consistency. Lewis was concerned with combining the rational and imaginative in such a way as to create a heightened perception of reality. This is true not only in his Christian apologetic works but in his literary analysis as well. And, of course, his own fictional works are an attempt to combine these two threads, fantasy and reason, in a new creative structure.

Lewis, although having no formal training in theology, possessed a great deal of knowledge of Christian doctrine which he learned studying Medieval and Renaissance literature. Long before he became a Christian Lewis had read deeply in Dante, Spenser, Milton, and George Herbert. Lewis also felt a strong debt to classical thought. He wrote, "To lose what I owe to Plato and Aristotle would be like the amputation of a limb."[10] After Lewis became interested in Christianity as such, rather than in writers who happened to be Christian, he studied the more specific theological works of St. Augustine, Richard Hooker, and Thomas Traherne. He also read William Law's Serious Call and Thomas a Kempis's Imitation of Christ. Lewis continued to acknowledge a conscious debt to these writers for the rest of his life.

Lewis saw the reading of older works as an advantage in rising above the "spirit of the age." Lewis felt that modern critics and theologians were often blinded by unconscious assumptions about reality of which they were completely unaware. Reading literature of other ages is one way to overcome this blindness toward one's own assumptions. Lewis commented: "It is a good rule, after reading a new book, never to allow yourself another new one till you have read an old one in-between."[11]

In his study of various controversies of the past, Lewis was struck by the fact that both sides were usually assuming without question a great deal that the modern age would totally deny. The opposing parties often saw themselves as complete opposites, where from a modern perspective it becomes obvious that they were in fact united with each other in basic world-view. Lewis observed: "They thought they were as completely opposed as two sides could be, but in fact they were all the time secretly united--united with each other and against earlier and later ages--by a great mass of common assumptions."[12]

Lewis felt that since past ages were often blind to their underlying assumptions, this must be true of our own age as well. Lewis wrote in 1943: "We may be sure that the characteristic blindness about which posterity will ask, 'But how could they have thought that?'--lies where we have never expected it, and concerns something about which there is untroubled agreement between Hitler and President Roosevelt, or between Mr. H. G. Wells and Karl Barth."[13]

None of us can totally escape the blindness of our own age, but Lewis felt that we can only increase it by reading solely modern works. It is not that people of other ages were more clever or less prone to make mistakes than we are now. But, although they made as many mistakes as modern men, they did not make the same mistakes. Their errors, Lewis said, will be open and obvious to us, thereby posing no threat. Their positive insights, on the other hand, may make us aware of weaknesses in our own assumptions that we had previously totally ignored.

Lewis found that in studying theologians of past ages he was better able to come to an understanding of the nature of Christianity than in studying modern writers. Thus, Lewis states: "If any man is tempted to think--as one might be tempted who read only contemporaries--that 'Christianity' is a word of so many meanings that it means nothing at all, he can learn beyond all doubt by stepping out of his own century, that this is not so. Measured against the ages 'mere Christianity' turns out to be no insipid interdenominational transparency, but something positive, self-consistent, and inexhaustible."[14]

Lewis's insistence on reason has led some critics to conclude that Lewis was essentially Thomistic in his theology. In a letter to Corbin Carnell, Lewis did not deny the profound influence of the Summa Theologica on his thought. In fact, Lewis admitted that for years he used the Summa as a kind of dictionary of medieval belief. But Lewis did not see Christianity as dependent on any philosophical system, although various systems have certainly lent themselves to interpreting the faith. Lewis declared that the appearance of a strong Thomistic influence was really due to the fact that he often, especially in the area of ethics, followed Aristotle where Aquinas also followed Aristotle. "Aquinas and I," Lewis admitted, "were in fact at the same school--I don't say in the same class! And I had read the Ethics long before I ever worked on the Summa."[15]

Even so, Lewis was not an uncritical admirer of Aristotle's approach to philosophy. He was strongly critical of it in his book The Allegory of Love. According to Lewis: "Aristotle is, before all, the philosopher of divisions. His effect on his greatest disciple (Aquinas), as M. Gilson has traced it, was to dig new chasms between God and the world, between human knowledge and reality, between faith and reason. Heaven began, under this dispensation, to seem far off. The danger of Pantheism grew less: the danger of mechanical Deism came a step nearer. It is almost as if the first, faint shadow of Descartes, or even of 'our present discontents' had fallen across the scene."[16]

Charles Hartshorne also noted Lewis's dissatisfaction with the Thomist doctrine of the "impassivity of God."[17] Hartshorne concluded that Lewis was a theologian steeped in the writings of the past but not slavishly reliant on them. Or, as Corbin Carnell observed: "My own reading of Lewis shows him to be Thomist, Aristotelian, Platonic, or Neo-Kantian (though rarely the latter) only as something in each of these approaches serves him as a tool of thought. I suspect that on the whole his tough-minded theology finds its logical sanctions in Aristotelian analysis. But one cannot say this without immediately balancing the statement with the observation that many aspects of Lewis's thought are Platonic to the core."[18]

Lewis admitted the need of balancing one's rational conclusions with intuitive insights. Rationalism alone can become sterile, missing the depths of human experience. As Lewis commented on his own position: "I am a rationalist. For me reason is the natural organ of truth; but imagination is the organ of meaning. Imagination, producing new metaphors or revivifying old, is not the cause of truth, but its condition."[19]

Although one must use reason to discuss anything intelligently, the nature of language requires that the highest truths be expressed in symbols which are imaginatively understood. According to Lewis, Kant and Spinoza, the great philosophical rationalists, may not have been so literal and unmystical as they thought. On the other hand, Plato, the great master of metaphor and author of the "myth of the cave," may have been the one with the higher percentage of meaning.

This tendency to read only theologians of other ages provided Lewis with both advantages and disadvantages in communicating Christian doctrine to his own age. While Lewis agreed at many points with writers like Kierkegaard, Maritain, and Berdyaev, he found them repetitive and ambiguous compared with the writings of earlier theologians. Because of this indifference, Lewis avoided becoming seriously entangled in the theological disputes and "fads" of his day. Thus, in many ways his writing seems less dated than that of contemporaries like J. A. T. Robinson or Harvey Cox. On the other hand, because Lewis's roots were primarily in older periods, he had little to contribute to those involved with Twentieth Century Existentialist Philosophy or to those involved in the Process Theology inspired by the philosophical world-view of Alfred North Whitehead.

Lewis showed a surprising lack of interest in much current theological writing, an indifference that sometimes betrayed a lack of understanding. As Lewis wrote in a private letter in 1961: "At the back of religious Existentialism lies Kierkegaard. They all revere him as their pioneer. Have you read him? I haven't, or hardly at all."[20] And again in another letter, "I can't read Kierkegaard myself, but some people find him helpful."[21]

Lewis did not appreciate the work of such contemporary theologians as Teilhard de Chardin, Paul Tillich, and especially Rudolf Bultmann. He was also strongly critical of the popularized versions of their work found in J. A. T. Robinson's book <u>Honest to God</u> (1963). Lewis wrote a biting review of the book shortly before his death. In the review Lewis commented that "most of us Christian laymen" had long ago abandoned the belief in a deity in a localized heaven who sits on a heavenly throne. He pointed out, with obvious relish, that this belief is called anthropomorphism. It was officially rejected during the early stages of Christianity, "there is something about this in Gibbon."[22] Lewis mockingly concluded: "If I were briefed to defend his <Robinson's> position, I should say 'The image of the Earth-Mother gets in something which that of the Sky-Father leaves out. Religions of the Earth-Mother have hitherto been spiritually inferior to those of the Sky-father, but, perhaps, it is now time to readmit some of their elements.' I shouldn't believe it very strongly, but some sort of case could be made out."[23] Lewis privately referred to Robinson, the Bishop of Woolwich, as "the Bishop of Woolworths'." As Lewis biographer Humphrey Carpenter points out: "To someone who had come to Christianity through a perception of its character as a myth, the notion of abandoning that myth was the ultimate absurdity."[24]

William White, a Lewis critic, has indicated that anyone familiar with the later Karl Barth will feel that Lewis's occasional remarks about Barthianism as "a flattening out of all things into common insignificance before the inscrutable Creator" are oversimplified and unfair. Although this criticism of the early Barth may be somewhat valid, by the time Barth wrote his essay <u>The Humanity of God</u> in 1956, his views were considerably changed. Thus by Lewis's "writing Barth off," Lewis missed the developments and subtleties of Barth's later work.[25]

Lewis did admire some modern theological writers, such as Martin Buber and Gabriel Marcel. Lewis was particularly indebted to Buber's <u>I and Thou</u> (1922); a debt Lewis freely admitted. As he stated in his last apologetic book, <u>Letters to Malcolm: Chiefly on</u>

Prayer: "The Person in Him--He is more than a Person--meets those who can welcome or at least face it. He speaks as 'I' when we truly call Him 'Thou' (How good Buber is!)."[26]

Lewis also admitted being strongly influenced by Rudolf Otto's book, The Idea of the Holy (1923). In that book Otto wrote of "a unique 'Wholly Other' reality and quality, something of whose special character we can feel without being able to give it clear conceptual expression."[27]

Lewis referred to man's basic awareness of the Divine (or the Holy) by using Otto's expression "the experience of the Numinous."[28] A common theme of both Otto's and Lewis's writing is that of fallen and finite humanity having cause to shrink in the presence of Divine Goodness. Lewis described such an encounter with "the Numinous" in his science fiction story Perelandra: "Here at last was a bit of that world from beyond the world, which I had always supposed that I loved and desired, breaking through and appearing to my senses: and I didn't like it, I wanted it to go away. I wanted every possible distance, gulf, curtain, blanket, and barrier to be placed between it and me."[29]

Lewis also at various times mentioned his appreciation of Anders Nygren's Agape and Eros(1953), G.K. Chesterton's Everlasting Man (1925), and Edwyn Bevan's Symbolism and Belief (1938). Lewis further mentioned learning from the writings of Carl Jung, particularly Jung's theory of the "collective unconscious."

Lewis understood Jung's doctrine of Primordial Images or Archetypal Patterns as being the description of a collective unconscious that is common to the whole human race and to some degree the whole animal world. Being pre-logical, its reactions are expressed not in thought but in images. The older and greater myths are such images recovered from the collective unconscious. As Jung perceived it, "Myths . . . consist of symbols that were not invented but happened. It was not the man Jesus who created the myth of the God man; it had existed many centuries before."[30]

Although Lewis suspended his judgement about the

scientific value of Jung's theory, Lewis commented, "I perceive at once that even if it turns out to be bad science it is excellent poetry."[31] Lewis and Jung also share a mutual suspicion of those who would attempt to "demythologize" Christianity.

Jung stated: "How, then can one possibly 'demythologize' the figure of Christ? . . . What is the use of a religion without a mythos, since religion means, if anything at all, precisely that function which links us back to the eternal myth?"[32]

Lewis pointed out that Jung's discussion of "primordial images" itself evokes a primordial image; "It might be called the Recovery Pattern, or the Veiled Isis, or the Locked Door, or the Lost and Found."[33] It is that primordial image that may explain the appeal of Jung's theory. Lewis concluded, "The mystery of primordial images is deeper, their origin more remote, their cave more hid, their fountain less accessible than those suspect who have yet dug deepest, sounded with the longest cord, or journeyed farthest in the wilderness."[34]

Of course, since Lewis never embraced the Liberal Protestantism of the late Nineteenth and early Twentieth Centuries, he did not find it necessary to react violently against a rationalistic approach in order to recover his faith. The Neo-Orthodox and Existentialist suspicions of the "pitfalls of rationalism" touched Lewis very little, since it was in large part the "tools of reason" that allowed Lewis to construct a believable faith.

Lewis's stress on the need to read Christian writers of past ages rather than modern ones has become somewhat ironic. Lewis himself has been praised as a writer who can communicate Christianity to "modern man."

Finally, Lewis also acknowledged the impact on his thought of a Nineteenth Century writer of Christian fantastic fiction, George MacDonald. At the end of February 1916 (Lewis mistakenly dates it August 1915 in <u>Surprised by Joy</u>) Lewis made one of the literary discoveries which was to leave the deepest and most enduring impression on both his literary and spiritual life. "I have had a great literary experience this week," he wrote his friend Arthur Greeves.

"I have discovered yet another author to add to our circle. . . . and indeed I think my new 'find' is quite as good as Malory or Morris himself. The book, to get to the point, is George MacDonald's 'Faerie Romance,' <u>Phantastes</u>, which I picked up by hazard in a rather tired Everyman copy on our station bookstall last Saturday."[35]

Thirty years later, in the introduction to an anthology of MacDonald's writings, Lewis commented: "I have never concealed the fact that I regard him as my master; indeed, I fancy I have never written a book in which I did not quote from him."[36] Lewis concluded: "Nothing was at that time <when he discovered MacDonald> further from my thoughts than Christianity. . . . What it <<u>Phantastes</u>> actually did to me was to convert, even to baptize. . . my imagination. It did nothing to my intellect nor (at that time) to my conscience. Their turn came far later and with the help of many other books and men."[37]

What Lewis found appealing in MacDonald's work was his ability to create modern myth. This is what Lewis himself attempted in much of his fantastic fiction. MacDonald was the first modern writer to show Lewis that this was possible. As he described it: "Most myths were made in prehistoric times, and I suppose, not consciously made by individuals at all. But every now and then there occurs in the modern world a genius--a Kafka or a Novalis--who can make such a story. MacDonald is the greatest genius of this kind whom I know."[38]

MacDonald opened Lewis's mind to the world beyond the logical. As Lewis was to remark, "The quality which had enchanted me in his imaginative works turned out to be the quality of the real universe, the divine, magical, and ecstatic reality in which we all live."[39] Of course, Lewis never totally rejected either the logical or the imaginative, but combined them in defense of a Christianity that he claimed was both, "myth become fact."

On a more personal level, Lewis also mentioned being strongly influenced by both teachers and friends. The teacher that had the most impact on Lewis was a man named W. T. Kirkpatrick, an Ulster Scottish schoolmaster at Bookham Surrey. Kirkpatrick privately tutored Lewis, beginning in 1914. Nicknamed the "Great Knock," Kirkpatrick was a stern atheist and a relentless logician. When Lewis first met his new teacher on arrival at the railway station, he attempted some small talk, remarking that the Surrey countryside was more wild than he expected. "Stop!" shouted Kirkpatrick. "What do you mean by wildness, and what ground had you for not expecting it?"[40] Lewis tried his best to answer, but every reply was rejected as inadequate. Finally, Kirkpatrick concluded: "Do you not see, then, that your remark was meaningless?"[41]

In the two years that Lewis studied with Kirkpatrick he learned to phrase all his remarks as logical propositions and to defend his opinions by argument. "No doubt I snorted and bridled a bit at some of my tossings," Lewis later remembered, "but all in all I loved the treatment."[42]

Although Lewis considered himself an atheist at this point in his life, this was not a direct result of Kirkpatrick's teaching. Lewis had begun to abandon his religious beliefs some years earlier, partly because as a child he found it impossible to make his prayers sincere, partly because he didn't think Christianity had much connection with the unhappy world around him, and partly because the Bible did not appeal to him as story.

As Lewis pointed out in his autobiography, "What I got there was merely fresh ammunition for the defense of a position already chosen. Even this I got indirectly from the tone of his <Kirkpatrick's> mind or independently from reading his books. He never attacked religion in my presence."[43]

Even after Lewis's rejection of atheism, he did not reject Kirkpatrick's approach to logic. Lewis described Kirkpatrick as a "Rationalist" of the old Nineteenth Century type, steeped in Frazer's The Golden Bough and Schopenhauer. As Lewis wrote in Surprised by Joy: "Atheism has come down in the world since those days, and mixed itself with politics and learned to dabble in dirt. The anonymous donor who now sends me anti-God magazines hopes, no doubt, to hurt the Christian in me; he really hurts the ex-atheist."[44] Lewis included an affectionate character sketch of the Scottish schoolmaster in his fictional MacPhee of That Hideous Strength, written long after

Lewis's conversion to Christianity. Lewis concluded his chapter on Kirkpatrick in Surprised by Joy with these words: "Kirk taught me Dialectic. . . . My debt to him is very great, my reverence to this day undiminished."[45]

In his later life, Lewis was influenced by his own circle of friends, particularly a group which called itself "The Inklings," a circle of literary friends with a common interest in writing and in discussing the nature of language and myth. Although membership in the group varied, it usually included J. R. R. Tolkien, Owen Barfield, Hugo Dyson, Fr. Gervase Matthew, and Charles Williams. Although the writer Dorothy Sayers was not a member of the group, she was closely associated with it through her friendship with Williams, and the Inklings were deeply influenced by her religious works. As Lewis said about her book The Man Born to Be King (1943): "I have re-read it in every Holy Week since it first appeared, and have never re-read it without being deeply moved."[46]

The Inklings met every Tuesday morning in a small Oxford pub from eleven o'clock until one and again on Thursday evenings in Lewis's college rooms. At times, various authors would read portions of their "works in progress" in order to receive criticism, praise, or suggestions. It was in this group that Tolkien read portions of his Lord of the Rings, Charles Williams his All Hallows Eve, and Lewis his The Great Divorce, Perelandra, and Screwtape Letters.

Lewis found the "romantic theology" of Charles Williams particularly appealing. Lewis defined William's romantic theology as follows: "A romantic theologian does not mean one who is romantic about theology, but one who is theological about romance; one who considers the theological implications of those experiences called romantic. The beliefs that the most serious and ecstatic experiences either of human love or of imaginative literature have such theological implications, and that they can be healthy and fruitful only if the implications are diligently sought out and severely lived, is the root principle of all his work."[47] Lewis was also influenced by Williams' "affirmative way," which stressed the transmutation of the delights of the world into the Christian vision.

Williams was more open to opposing points of view than Lewis. Lewis called him "a rebunker," but William's influence seems to have softened Lewis's own approach. It is interesting to note that Lewis apologized in the second edition of The Pilgrim's Regress for the bitterness of his attacks. It is possible that Lewis would not have noticed the harshness of his attacks had it not been for his association with Williams. Lewis himself admitted that Williams had a way of showing the complexities of any intellectual position: "He excelled at showing you the little grain of truth or felicity in some passage generally quoted for ridicule, while at the same time he fully enjoyed the absurdity: or contrariwise, at detecting the little falsity or dash of silliness in a passage which you, and he also, admired."[48]

Another Inkling that influenced Lewis was Owen Barfield, Lewis's friend and intellectual opponent for over forty years. Barfield's attacks on "chronological snobbery," his belief that the spiritual life is immanent in phenomena, his views on the need of knowing through the imagination, and his view of thought as part of a larger extra-personal process- all had a strong impact on Lewis's beliefs.[49]

Still, Barfield was an Anthroposophist, and Lewis disagreed with certain points of Barfield's theology. Lewis and Barfield wrote a series of correspondences which they ironically nicknamed "the Great War." In particular, Lewis was uncomfortable with Barfield's notion that God himself undergoes an evolution of consciousness, and that specific religious observances were not necessary. Nevertheless, Barfield's insights made Lewis re-examine a number of his own prejudices, and provided several of the intellectual stepping stones in Lewis's conversion to Christianity.

Finally, Lewis was influenced by the Inkling and fantasy writer, J. R. R. Tolkien. It was Tolkien's interpretation of myth as fragments of eternal truth that allowed Lewis to see the truth in what he considered the Christian "myth."

Tolkien also influenced Lewis with his concept that in writing stories man is not a creator, but a sub-creator, who may hope to reflect something of the eternal light of God. Tolkien further gave Lewis an appreciation for the uses of fantasy to portray a deeper level of reality. As Lewis remarked in a review of Tolkien's <u>Lord of the Rings</u>, "One of the main things the author wants to say is that the real life of men is of that mythical and heroic quality. Much that in a realistic work would be done by 'character delineation' is here done simply by making the character an elf, a dwarf, or a hobbit. The imagined beings have their insides on the outside, they are visible souls. And Man as a whole, Man pitted against the universe, have we seen him at all till we see that he is like a hero in a fairy tale?"[50]

    The intellectual influences on Lewis's life include both classical writers and modern fantasy writers. Those who personally influenced Lewis include the logical atheist and the romantic theologian. But, of course, Lewis's own work is more than the sum of the influences on his life. In particular, it was his conversion to Christianity which gave him the means to filter these influences into a new creative synthesis. It is to the events leading up to that conversion that we now turn.

NOTES: CHAPTER ONE

[1] Chad Walsh ed., *The Visionary Christian* (New York: Macmillan, 1981), pp. 3-4. Walsh also published the first book devoted wholly to Lewis's life and work, *C. S. Lewis: Apostle to the Skeptics* (New York: The Macmillan Co., 1949). Other standard works on Lewis's life include Roger Lancelyn Green and Walter Hooper, *C. S. Lewis: A Biography* (New York: Harcourt Brace Jovanovich, 1974); Humphrey Carpenter, *The Inklings: C. S. Lewis, J. R. R. Tolkien, Charles Williams, and Their Friends* (Boston: Houghton Mifflin, 1978); and Lewis's autobiography, *Surprised by Joy: The Shape of My Early Life* (New York: Harcourt Brace and World, 1956). A recent biography written specifically for an American audience is William Griffin's *C. S. Lewis: A Dramatic Life* (San Francisco: Harper and Row, 1986).

[2] Chad Walsh, Afterword, in *A Grief Observed,* by C. S. Lewis (New York: Bantam Books, 1976), p. 120.

[3] C. S. Lewis, ed., *Essays Presented to Charles Williams* (Grand Rapids: William B. Eerdmans, 1966), p. xiii.

[4] C. S. Lewis, "Preface to the Paperback Edition," *The Screwtape Letters: with Screwtape Proposes a Toast* (New York: Macmillan paperback, 1975), p. v.

[5] Lewis, *Screwtape*, p. xiv.

[6] G. E. M. Anscombe, *The Collected Philosophical Papers of G.E.M. Anscombe* (Oxford: Basil Blackwell, 1981), II, pp. x, 224-231.

[7] Humphrey Carpenter, *The Inklings*, p. 223.

[8] C. S. Lewis, "De Descriptione Temporum," in his *Selected Literary Essays*, ed. Walter Hooper (Cambridge University Press, 1969), p. 14.

[9] C. S. Lewis, *An Experiment in Criticism* (Cambridge University Press, 1961), p. 141.

[10] Corbin S. Carnell, *Bright Shadow of Reality: C. S. Lewis and the Feeling Intellect* (Grand Rapids: William B. Eerdmans, 1974), pp. 68-69.

[11] C. S. Lewis, "On the Reading of Old Books," in his *God in the Dock,* ed. Walter Hooper (Grand Rapids: William B. Eerdmans, 1970), pp. 201-202.

[12] Lewis, *God in the Dock*, p. 202.

[13] Lewis, *God in the Dock*, p. 202.

[14] Lewis, *God in the Dock*, p. 203

[15] Carnell, *Bright Shadow of Reality*, p.71.

[16] C. S. Lewis, *The Allegory of Love: A Study in Medieval Tradition* (London: Oxford University Press, 1936), p. 88.

[17] Charles Hartshorne, "Philosophy and Orthodoxy," *Ethics*, 54 (July 1944), pp. 295-298.

[18] Carnell, *Bright Shadow of Reality*, p. 71.

[19] C.S. Lewis, "Bluspels and Flalansferes: A Semantic Nightmare," *Selected Literary Essays*, p. 265.

[20] "To a Lady," February, 1961, *Letters of C.S. Lewis*, ed. W. H. Lewis (New York: Harcourt Brace Jovanovich, 1966), p. 298.

[21] "To Mrs. Margaret Grey," May 9, 1961, *Letters of C.S.Lewis*, p. 184.

[22] C. S. Lewis, "Must Our Image of God Go?," *God in the Dock*, p. 184.

[23] Lewis, *God in the Dock,*, p. 185.

[24] Carpenter, *The Inklings*, p. 176.

[25] William Luther White, *The Image of Man in C. S. Lewis* (Nashville: Abingdon Press, 1969), p. 37.

[26] C. S. Lewis, *Letters to Malcolm: Chiefly on Prayer* (New York: Harcourt Brace Jovanovich, 1964), p. 21

[27] Rudolf Otto, *The Idea of the Holy* (London: Oxford University Press, 1923), p. 30.

²⁸C. S. Lewis, The Problem of Pain (New York: Macmillan paperback, 1961), p. 4.

²⁹C. S. Lewis, Perelandra (New York: Macmillan paperback, 1965), pp. 18-19.

³⁰C. G. Jung, "The Function of Religious Symbols," The Symbolic Life: Miscellaneous Writings, trans. by R. F. C. Hull, Bollingen Series XX (Princeton: Princeton University Press, 1976), p. 247.

³¹C. S. Lewis, "Psycho-Analysis and Literary Criticism," Selected Literary Essays, p. 297.

³²C. G. Jung, "Answer to Job," Psychology and Religion: West and East, Second Edition, trans. by R. F. C. Hull, Bollingen Series XX (Princeton: Princeton University Press, 1969), pp. 408-409.

³³Lewis, Selected Literary Essays, p. 299.

³⁴Lewis, Selected Literary Essays, p. 300.

³⁵Green and Hooper, C.S. Lewis: A Biography, p. 44.

³⁶C. S. Lewis, ed., George MacDonald: An Anthology (New York: The Macmillan Co., 1947), p. xxxii.

³⁷Lewis, MacDonald, p. xxxiii.

³⁸Lewis, MacDonald, p. xxviii.

³⁹Lewis, MacDonald, p. xxxiv.

⁴⁰C. S. Lewis, Surprised by Joy p. 134.

⁴¹Lewis, Surprised, p. 134.

⁴²Lewis, Surprised, p. 137.

⁴³Lewis, Surprised, p. 140.

⁴⁴Lewis, Surprised, p. 139.

⁴⁵Lewis, Surprised, p. 148.

⁴⁶C. S. Lewis, "A Panegyric for Dorothy Sayers," in his On Stories: and Other Essays on Literature, ed. Walter Hooper (New York: Harcourt Brace Jovano-

vich, 1982), p. 93.

⁴⁷Lewis, Essays Presented to Charles Williams, p. vi.

⁴⁸Lewis, Essays To Williams, p. xi.

⁴⁹Carpenter, The Inklings, p. 163.

⁵⁰Lewis, "Tolkien's The Lord of the Rings," On Stories, p. 89.

CHAPTER TWO

LEWIS'S CONVERSION TO "MYTH BECOME FACT"

C. S. Lewis was not always a Christian believer. His early views of Christianity can be summed up in a letter he wrote to his friend Arthur Greeves on October 12, 1916:

>You ask me my religious views: you know, I think that I believe in no religion. There is absolutely no proof for any of them, and from a philosophical standpoint Christianity is not even the best. All religions, that is, all mythologies to give them their proper name, are merely man's own invention--Christ as much as Loki. Primitive man found himself surrounded by all sorts of terrible things he didn't understand--thunder, pestilence, snakes etc.: what more natural than to suppose that these were animated by evil spirits trying to torture him. These he kept off by cringing to them, singing songs, and making sacrifices etc. Gradually, from being mere nature-spirits these supposed being(s) were elevated into more elaborate ideas, such as the old gods, and when man became more refined he pretended that these spirits were good as well as powerful.
>
>Thus religion, that is to say mythology, grew up. Often, too, great men were regarded as gods after their death--such as Heracles or Odin: thus after the death of a Hebrew philosopher Yeshua (whose name we have corrupted into Jesus) he became regarded as a god, a cult sprang up, which was afterwards connected with the ancient Hebrew Jahweh worship, and so Christianity came into being--one mythology among many, but the one that we happen to have been brought up in.[1]

To the adolescent Lewis, Christianity had come to mean ugly architecture, ugly music, and bad poetry, plus a God whom Lewis saw as the "Transcendental Interferer." He later commented on this period of his life in <u>Surprised by Joy</u>: "I exulted with youthful and vulgar pride in what I thought my enlightenment . . . . I was in that state of mind in which a boy thinks it extremely telling to call God 'Jahweh' and Jesus 'Yeshua.'"[2]

Nevertheless, in the same letter cited above in which Lewis attacked Christianity so vehemently, Lewis concluded: "Of course, mind you, I am not laying down as a certainty that there is nothing outside the material world: considering the discoveries that are always being made, this would be foolish. The answer is yet to seek. Whenever any new light can be got as to such matters, I will be glad to welcome it."[3]

It seems that new light was shed on such matters. As Lewis later confessed, "The Things I assert most vigorously are those that I resisted long and accepted late."[4] It was at this point in Lewis's life that he read George MacDonald's <u>Phantastes.</u> Alongside the romantic elements in the novel, Lewis found something new. It was a "bright shadow" that he later discovered to be the voice of holiness: "something too near to see, too plain to be understood, on this side of knowledge."[5]

At the age of eighteen, Lewis took the scholarship examination for Oxford, was elected, and entered in the summer of 1917. However, World War I was grinding slowly to a close, and Lewis felt duty-bound to enlist before his first term was up. At nineteen, Lewis was in the front-line trenches in France as a second lieutenant. A brief illness resulted in a three week stay in an army hospital. There Lewis first began to read G. K. Chesterton. He loved Chesterton in spite of Chesterton's Christianity. As Lewis later remembered, he came to feel "Christians are wrong, but all the rest are bores."[6]

Lewis was wounded at the front in April, 1918. In January 1919 he was discharged from military service. Lewis returned to Oxford in 1919 where he embarked upon the Honors School of Classics known as "Greats."

Lewis made friends with several individuals whose religious beliefs also began to influence him. It was at Oxford that he first met Owen Barfield who destroyed Lewis's belief in "chronological snobbery." Barfield showed Lewis that abstract thought can give indisputable truth of a different sort from the experience of the senses. Barfield finally convinced Lewis that logic itself participated in a cosmic "Logos," a cosmic Absolute. At this point Lewis still did not assume that the Absolute was a "Personal" Being.

Lewis finally completed "Greats" in 1922 and then took a fourth year, this time in the English School. Here, Lewis made friends with a classmate named Nevill Coghill who was not only "the most intelligent and best informed man in that class," but was also "a Christian, and a thorough-going supernaturalist."[7]

Lewis began to find his literary interests turning more and more toward Christian writers-- MacDonald, Chesterton, Dr. Johnson, Spenser, Milton. Lewis later described this period: "I must have been as blind as a bat not to have seen, long before, the ludicrous contradiction between my theory of life and my actual experience as a reader."[8]

Even the pagan writers which he enjoyed-Plato, Aeschylus, Virgil--seemed also to be the most religious. Those writers that in theory he should have been most sympathetic with--George Bernard Shaw, H. G. Wells, John Stuart Mill, Gibbon, Voltaire--all seemed to Lewis "a little thin" or "tinny." As he saw it, "There seemed to be no depth in them. They were too simple. The roughness and density of life did not appear in their books."[9]

Eventually, although Lewis still thought of Christianity as only a myth, he felt it was a good framework on which to hang Absolute Idealism. According to Lewis, "I thought that 'the Christian myth' conveyed to unphilosophic minds as much of the truth, that is of Absolute Idealism, as they were capable of grasping, and that even that much put them above the irreligious."[10]

In 1924, Lewis became a temporary lecturer in Philosophy at University College and also served gin the role of "tutor." A year later, at the age of twenty-six, Lewis was elected a Fellow of Magdalen College. He was later to receive his Master of Arts and become a special lecturer.

Lewis now became friends with J. R. R. Tolkien who was both a Roman Catholic and a philologist--two things Lewis had previously mistrusted. Lewis also began to reread Euripides' <u>Hippolytus</u>, and this introduced in him a state of intense longing that he had previously experienced at various crucial points in his boyhood. Lewis came to describe this longing as <u>Sehnsucht</u>, which Lewis creatively translated as "Joy."

Although Lewis had felt these inexpressible longings as a child, he had come to believe he had outgrown them. But, surprisingly, the longings persisted. As Lewis was later to describe them:

> Most people, if they had really learned to look into their own hearts, would know that they do want and want acutely, something that cannot be had in this world. There are all sorts of things in this world that offer to give it to you, but they never quite keep their promise. The longings which arise in us when we first fall in love, or first think of some foreign country, or first take up some subject that excites us, are longings which no marriage, no travel, no learning, can really satisfy.[11]

Shortly after this experience Lewis read Samuel Alexander's <u>Space, Time, and Deity</u> (1920). There Lewis found a distinction between enjoyment and contemplation that helped him make sense of his feelings. According to Alexander, one "enjoys" the act of thinking and "contemplates" whatever it is one is thinking about. For example, Lewis discovered that the essential property of love is attention to the beloved. To think about not the beloved but loving itself is to enjoy your own thoughts and to cease attending to the object of these thoughts.[12]

Thus, if we try to look "inside ourselves" and watch what is going on, nearly everything that was going on before we looked is stopped. As a result, the experience of <u>Sehnsucht</u> or Joy is not an end in itself. It is a reminder or pointer to something else--something far more desirable than the sensations that accompany this desire.

But what is the object of this desire? According to Lewis, if one finds in oneself a desire which no experience can satisfy, the most probable explanation is that one was made for another world. As Lewis argues: "If none of my earthly pleasures can satisfy it, that does not prove that the universe is a fraud. Probably earthly pleasures were never meant to satisfy it, but only to arouse it, to suggest the real thing."[13] In other words, these "immortal longings" which Lewis experienced were, in Peter Berger's phrase, "signals of transcendence." They implied the existence of a realm beyond the material world. Otherwise, Lewis believed, the feelings or longings themselves would be absurd.

Eventually, Lewis came to see that we yearn for that Absolute, called "God," beside which we are mere "appearances." While Lewis was a temporary lecturer in philosophy, he found that such philosophical idealists as Hegel and F. H. Bradley were vague on their meaning of the term "Absolute." On the other hand, Lewis found the theistic idealism of George Berkeley more persuasive because it was easier to get some notion of what Berkeley's "God" was.

Still, Lewis felt that he had committed himself only to the acceptance of, as Pascal phrased it, "the God of the philosophers," not the God of popular religion: "I distinguished this philosophical 'God' very sharply (or so I said) from 'the God of popular religion.' There was, I explained, no possibility of being in a personal relationship to Him. . . . I didn't call Him 'God' either, I called Him 'Spirit.' One fights for one's remaining comforts."[14]

It was at this point in Lewis's life that he read G. K. Chesterton's <u>Everlasting Man</u>. For the first time Lewis saw that the whole Christian outline of history seemed to make sense. Chesterton's book would have a continuing impact on Lewis for the rest of his life, even though he ultimately rejected Chesterton's acceptance of Roman Catholicism.

Then, in an incident that had a profound influence on Lewis, he was confronted with the historical nature of Christianity in a more personal way. Lewis described the incident in his autobiography:

> Early in 1926 the hardest boiled of all the atheists I ever knew sat in my room on the other side of the fire and remarked that the evidence for the historicity of the Gospels was really surprisingly good. "Rum thing," he went on. "All that stuff of Frazer's about the Dying God. Rum thing. It almost looks as if it had really happened once." To understand the shattering impact of it, you would need to know the man (who has certainly never since showed any interest in Christianity). If he, the cynic of cynics, the toughest of toughs, were not, as I would still have put it--"safe," where could I turn? Was there then no escape?[15]

After this, Lewis's conversion took on a certain inevitability. But it was not a conversion entered into without reluctance. As Lewis wrote to his friend Owen Barfield in 1929: "Terrible things are happening to me. The 'Spirit' or 'Real I' is showing an alarming tendency to become much more personal and is taking the offensive and behaving just like God. You'd better come on Monday at the latest or I may have entered a monastery."[16]

Lewis became aware of a personal element in what he had so far accepted only intellectually. As he related it: "I was going up Headington Hill on the top of a bus. Without words and (I think) almost without images, a fact about myself was presented to me. I became aware that I was holding something at bay, or shutting something out."[17]

Lewis was still hoping that he might not be "interfered with," that he would be allowed to retain his freedom. But it was not to be. Lewis revealed in his autobiography what happened:

> You must picture me alone in that room in Magdalen, night after night, feeling, whenever my mind lifted even for a second from my work the steady, unrelenting approach of Him whom I so earnestly desired not to meet. That

which I greatly feared had at last come upon me. In the Trinity term of 1929 I gave in, and admitted that God was God, and knelt and prayed: perhaps the most dejected and reluctant convert in all England."[18]

This conversion was to theism, however, not Christianity. Lewis did begin to attend church on Sunday. This was despite his distaste for the "public" aspect of church-going and his more intense dislike of organ music, which he once described to Walter Hooper as "one long roar."

Lewis also began reading John's Gospel in the Greek, beginning a practice that was to continue for the rest of his life. From then on, Lewis would read some portion of the Bible almost every day. Although he got a more balanced view of Christ than he had in 1916 when he described Jesus as a "Hebrew Philosopher," he was troubled by the Gospels' divergences from the popular conceptions of Jesus. Lewis wrote his friend Arthur Greeves on January 9, 1930: "In spite of all my recent change of views, I am . . . inclined to think that you can only get what you call 'Christ' out of the Gospels by picking and choosing, and slurring over a great deal."[19]

Though he continued to argue Christian doctrine with friends like Tolkien and Barfield, Lewis said very little to friends from his undergraduate period about the change he was going through. An exception was A. K. Hamilton Jenkins, to whom Lewis confessed in a letter dated March 21, 1930 that his outlook had changed considerably since their undergraduate days: "It is not precisely Christianity, though it may turn out that way in the end. I can't express the change better than by saying that whereas once I would have said 'Shall I adopt Christianity?', I now wait to see whether it will adopt me: i.e. I now know there is another Party in the affair--that I'm playing poker, not patience, as I once supposed."[20]

Finally, on September 19, 1931, Lewis invited Tolkien and Hugo Dyson to dine with him. Henry Victor Dyson, always known as "Hugo," lectured on English Literature at Reading University. He was two years older than Lewis and had been severely wounded in World War I. Dyson had also read English at Oxford and was a practicing member of the Church of England. Lewis had been introduced to Dyson in July 1930 by Nevill Coghill, had taken to him immediately, and had found Dyson to be both a philosopher and a religious man. Following an after-dinner walk, Lewis, Tolkien, and Dyson spent the whole night talking in Lewis's room.

A few days later (October 1), Lewis wound up a long letter to Arthur Greeves with the news: "I have just passed on from believing in God to definitely believing in Christ--in Christianity. I will try to explain this another time. My long night talk with Dyson and Tolkien had a great deal to do with it."[21]

Soon afterwards, on October 18, 1931, Lewis wrote to his old friend Greeves again and described what had happened that night:

> What Dyson and Tolkien showed me was this: that if I met the idea of sacrifice in a pagan story I didn't mind it at all: again, that if I met the idea of a god sacrificing himself to himself. . . I liked it very much and was mysteriously moved by it: again, that the idea of the dying and reviving god (Balder, Adonis, Bacchus) similarly moved me provided I met it anywhere <u>except</u> in the Gospels. The reason was that in pagan stories I was prepared to feel the myth as profound and suggestive of meanings beyond my grasp even tho' I could not say in cold prose "what it meant." Now the story of Christ is simply a true myth: a myth working on us in the same way as the others, but with this tremendous difference, that it really <u>happened</u>.[22]

This conception of "myth become fact" would be a major element in Lewis's defense of Christian belief. Lewis, in <u>Surprised by Joy</u>, wrote that his final conclusions concerning the truth of Christianity had been made even before his letter to Greeves. On September 28, 1931, Lewis and his brother Warren had taken a picnic lunch to Whipsnade Zoo. Lewis related what followed: "When we set out I

34

did not believe that Jesus Christ is the Son of God, and when we reached the zoo I did. Yet I had not exactly spent the journey in thought. Nor in great emotion. 'Emotional' is perhaps the last word we can apply to some of the most important events. It was more like when a man, after a long sleep, still lying motionless in bed, becomes aware that he is now awake."[23]

Actually, Lewis's conversion may not have been quite so sudden as his autobiography indicated. After Arthur Greeves wrote to Lewis saying he was delighted that his friend had at last accepted Christianity, Lewis began to feel that "perhaps I had said too much." He went on: "Perhaps I was not nearly as clear on the subject as I led you to think. But I certainly have moved <u>a bit</u>, even if it turns out to be less a bit than I thought."[24]

As Humphrey Carpenter has pointed out, "Lewis had reached the point where rational argument failed, and it became a matter of belief rather than of logical proof."[25] Lewis realized the need for some sort of "leap of faith" to get over the final hurdle. "There must," he said, "perhaps always be just enough lack of demonstrative certainty to make free choice possible, for what could we do but accept if the faith were like the multiplication table?"[26]

So Lewis became a Christian and made his Communion for the first time since his childhood on Christmas Day, 1931, in his parish church at Headington Quarry. Even after his conversion, there were, he later admitted, many moments when he felt "How could I--I of all people--ever have come to believe this cock-and-bull story?"[27] But Lewis felt his attitude was better than taking his faith for granted. Nor was he totally shocked by the idea that Christianity might, after all, be untrue. "Even assuming (which I most constantly deny) that the doctrines of historical Christianity are merely mythical," Lewis later wrote, "it is the myth which is the vital and nourishing element in the whole concern."[28]

Lewis's new attitude to myth can be found in <u>The Pilgrim's Regress: An Allegorical Apology for Christianity, Reason, and Romanticism</u>, written less than a year after he had become a Christian. Lewis already felt capable of telling other people about his own experiences, becoming an "apologist," a defender of Christianity by argument.

Lewis was, of course, modeling his book on Bunyan's <u>Pilgrim's Progress</u>. Though he never used allegory in any of his other books, he found that it provided a sudden release for what he wanted to say. Like Bunyan's, the account is set forth as a dream in which the hero undergoes perilous adventures, representing a man in search of Joy, which in the end turns out to be a search for God.

At one point in the story, the pilgrim John, troubled by the mythological nature of Christianity, hears a voice, declaring:

> Child, if you will, it <u>is</u> mythology. It is but truth, not fact: an image, not the very real. But since they do not know themselves for what they are, in them the hidden myth is master, where it would be servant: and it is but of man's inventing. But this is My inventing, this is the veil under which I have chosen to appear even from the first until now. For this end I made your senses and for this end your imagination, that you might see My face and live. What would you have? Have you not heard among the Pagans the story of Semele? Or was there any age in any land when men did not know that corn and wine were the blood and body of a dying and yet living God?[29]

Lewis's view of myth as found in this passage seems to derive in part from the conversation Lewis had with Tolkien on September 19, 1931. On that eventful night, Lewis described myths as "lies and therefore worthless, even though breathed through silver." But Tolkien replied, "No. They are not lies." Tolkien went on:

> You look at trees, and call them "trees" and probably you do not think twice about the word. You call a star "a star," and think nothing more of it. But you must remember that these words, "tree," "star," were (in their original forms) names given to these objects by

people with very different views from yours. To you, a tree is simply a vegetable organism, and a star simply a ball of inanimate matter moving along a mathematical course. But the first men to talk of "trees" and "stars" saw things very differently. To them, the world was alive with mythological beings. They saw the stars as living silver, bursting into flame in answer to the eternal music. They saw the sky as a jewelled tent, and the earth as the womb whence all living things have come. To them, the whole of creation was "myth-woven and elf-patterned."[30]

Tolkien developed this theme further. He declared that not only the abstract thoughts of man but also his imaginative inventions must originate with God, and must in consequence reflect something of eternal truth. In making a myth, the story teller or "sub-creator" (that is, one under God, the prime Creator), is actually fulfilling God's purpose and reflecting a splintered fragment of the true light. Pagan myths are therefore never just "lies": there is always something of truth in them.[31]

Lewis attempted to describe to his friend Arthur Greeves the new insights he had obtained through his conversation with Tolkien. Lewis achieved a new view of both pagan mythology and Christianity, seeing the underlying component of myth as the common element between them. According to Lewis: "The Pagan stories are God expressing Himself through the minds of poets, using such images as He found there, while Christianity is God expressing Himself through what we call 'real things.' Therefore it is *true*, not in the sense of being 'a description' in which God chooses to (or can) appear to our faculties. The 'doctrines' we get *out of* true myth are of course *less* true: they are translations into our *concepts* and *ideas* of that which God has already expressed in a language more adequate, namely the actual incarnation, crucifixion and resurrection."[32]

In other words, when Divine Truth falls on human imagination, myth is born. Myth puts us in touch with Reality in a more intimate way than by knowing what is merely factual. Myth touches our lives at a deeper level than abstract thought and thus, is the best means of Divine communication.

Lewis stated that myth should not be confused with mere allegory. In allegory, the images stand for concepts. In myth, the images symbolize and imagine <u>something</u> which cannot be reduced to a concept. Allegory can always be translated back into meaningful concepts. Mythical meaning cannot be fully stated in conceptual terms.[33]

In its fullest sense, myth is extra-literary. According to Lewis, myth does not exist in words at all. It can be distinguished from the language structures in which it is expressed. As Lewis revealed in his book <u>An Experiment in Criticism</u>: "It is true that such a story can hardly reach us except in words. But this is logically accidental. If some perfected art of mime or silent film or serial pictures could make it clear with no words at all, it would still affect us in the same way."[34]

Myth also has an element of fantasy or the "fantastic," which cannot be related in a simplistic fashion to the every-day world. As Lewis argued: "Myth is always, in one sense of that word, 'fantastic.' It deals with impossibles and preternaturals."[35] A mythic fantasy is a type of fairy tale which implies "I am merely a work of art. You must take me as such--must enjoy me for my suggestions, my beauty, my irony, my construction and so forth. There is no question of anything like this happening in the real world."[36] As one critic commented on Lewis's view of myth: "myths have meaning not to those who insist on literal truth, but to those who have spiritual eyes to see and ears to hear the truth conveyed through myth."[37]

Another characteristic of myth is that it embodies universal reality. However, the actual reality of which myth is only an image is always greater than the abstract meaning extracted from the myth through analysis. What flows from myth, said Lewis, is not truth, but reality. Truth is always about something, whereas reality is that <u>about which</u> truth is. The moment the truth embodied in myth is stated in conceptual-verbal form, a lesser abstraction results. According to Lewis, "It is only while receiving the myth as story that you experience the principle concretely."[38]

Every myth can become the father of innumerable truths on the abstract level. Using an image from geography, Lewis states that myth is "the isthmus which connects the peninsular world of thought with that vast continent we really belong to. It is not, like truth, abstract; nor is it, like direct experience, bound to the particular."[39] The reality found in myth cannot be put into words or grasped by the intellect alone. It must be imagined or experienced.

Myth also has a unifying effect on the receiver. It evokes powerful emotional responses, such as awe, enchantment, and inspiration. Myths for Lewis served a purpose similar to the koans of Zen Buddhism, allowing their images to "register beneath the surface of the mind, allowing us to actually experience Reality and grasp eternal truths which might baffle the intellect and confuse the mind."[40]

Lewis was aware of the very deep level at which myth affects the recipient, having from his youth been moved by the power of Norse mythology. For Lewis at the age of thirteen, a translated passage of <u>Tegner's Drapa</u> which read "I heard a voice that cried,/ Balder the beautiful/ Is dead, is dead," awakened in him for the first time the desire he described as Joy (<u>Sehnsucht</u>). It was the attempt to meet this desire that drove him first to a fascination with mythology and later to a commitment to Christianity. As Lewis testified, myth is capable of arousing much in us: "sensations we have never had before, never anticipated having, as though we had broken out of our normal mode of consciousness and 'possessed joys not promised to our birth.' It gets under our skin, hits us at a deeper level than our thoughts or even our passions, troubles oldest certainties till all questions are re-opened, and in general shocks us more fully awake than we are for most of our lives."[41]

Finally, myth serves as a bridge between the infinite realm of Absolute Reality and the finite realm of abstract, propositional truth. For Lewis the desire to investigate myth objectively has genuine attraction. But this attraction, he states, "springs in part from the same impulse that makes men allegorize the myths. It is one more effort to seize, to conceptualize, the important something which the myth seems to suggest."[42] Therefore, although we can analyze myth abstractly, we must never confuse the analysis with the myth itself.

But what does Lewis's concept of myth in general have to do with the nature of the Christian "myth?" When Lewis converted to Christianity, he became convinced that at the heart of Christianity is a myth which is also a fact. The old myth of the Dying God, <u>without ceasing to be myth</u>, "comes down from the heaven of legend and imagination to the earth of history. It <u>happens</u> at a particular date, in a particular place, followed by definable historical consequences."[43]

Rather than describing a legendary Balder or Osiris who died--nobody knows when or where--Christianity tells us of a person crucified in definite time and location, under the rule of a historical figure, Pontius Pilate. By becoming fact, Christianity does not cease to be myth. "Just as God is none the less God by being Man, so the Myth remains Myth, even when it becomes Fact. The story of Christ demands from us, and repays, not only a religious and historical, but also an imaginative response. It is directed to the child, the poet, and the savage in us as well as to the conscience and to the intellect. One of its functions is to break down dividing walls."[44]

As a result of this view of myth, Lewis found the parallels in pagan mythology to the Christian story not as disconcerting similarities but as affirming signs of the truth of the Christian message. Lewis declared that Christians must not be ashamed of the "parallels" and "pagan christs". They <u>ought to be there</u>. Lewis felt it would be more threatening to the Christian faith if these parallels were <u>not</u> there. As Lewis denoted the similarities between certain pagan myths and the Christian one: "The resemblance between these myths and the Christian truth is no more accidental than the resemblance between the sun and the sun's reflection in a pond. . . or between the trees and hills of the real world and the trees and hills of our dreams."[45]

As a result of Lewis's view of myth, he believed that our conceptions of God are determined by the images through which His revelation appears. Finite beings in a finite realm have no absolute knowledge of the Infinite God, only analogies, mythical models, symbols, and abstractions. As Lewis claimed: "Statements about God are extrapolations from knowledge of other things which the divine illumination enables us to know."[46]

Consequently, what we call "God" cannot be conceived apart from metaphoric images. A man who says "I do not believe in a personal God but I do believe in a great spiritual force," has through the use of his term "force" let in all types of images about winds, tides, electricity, and gravitation. When one refuses to describe God in personal terms but believes all men are part of one "Great Being," one has simply exchanged the image of a fatherly, royal-looking man for the image of a widely extended gas or fluid. Lewis told of a girl he knew who was brought up by "higher thinking" parents to regard God as a perfect "substance." In her later life she realized that this image had in fact made her conceive of God as something like a "vast tapioca pudding."[47]

Lewis concluded that all conceptions of God are accompanied by vague images which cannot be taken literally. If this were done, said Lewis, those "philosophic" conceptions of God would, if pushed to extremes, "turn out to be even more absurd than the man-like images aroused by Christian theology."[48]

In <u>The Pilgrim's Regress,</u> Lewis developed the theme that God revealed himself to Israel, "the Shepherd People," through the Law. He contrasted that approach with God's revelation to the pagans. For the pagans, "the Landlord <God> has circulated other things besides the Rules," the pilgrim John is told. "What use are Rules to people who cannot read."[49]

For the "illiterate," or pagans, God reveals himself in "pictures" or myths. Because these myths or "pictures" come from God, many pagans catch a glimpse of the Divine Order. The difference between pagan myths of redemption and Christianity "is not the difference between falsehood and truth. It is the difference between a real event on the one hand and dim dreams or premonitions of that same event on the other."[50]

Lewis further explained this view of pagan

mythology in <u>Miracles: A Preliminary Study</u>. Christ is like the corn-kings of pagan mythology, Lewis declared, "because the Corn-King is a portrait of Him. The similarity is not in the least unreal or accidental. For the Corn-King is derived (through human imagination) from the facts of Nature, and the facts of Nature from her Creator: the Death and Re-birth pattern is in her because it was first in Him."[51]

Lewis believed that one of the functions of the natural world is to furnish symbols that point to spiritual reality. Nature supplies the substance for myth; God supplies the meaning: "In the sequence of night and day, in the annual death and rebirth of the crops, in the myths which these processes gave rise to, in the strong, if half-articulate feeling (embodied in many pagan 'Mysteries') that man himself must undergo some sort of death if he would truly live, there is already a likeness permitted by God to that truth on which all depends."[52]

Lewis did not see all pagan mythology as a foreshadowing of the Christ event. "If we go steadily through all the myths of any people, we shall be appalled by much of what we read. Most of them, whatever they may have meant to ancient or savage man, are to us meaningless and shocking; shocking not only by their cruelty and obscenity, but by their apparent silliness--almost what seems insanity."[53] It is out of this "rank and squalid undergrowth," stated Lewis, that the great myths--those of Orpheus, Demeter and Persephone, of the Hesperides, and Balder--arise. And it is in the numerous myths of a dying and rising God that the final actualization of this myth in Christianity is foreshadowed.

So, as Lewis argued in <u>Pilgrim's Regress</u>, the "Shepherds" had their "Rules" and the pagans their "pictures." Still, each group possessed only part of the truth. As Lewis saw it: "The truth is that a Shepherd is only half a man, and a Pagan is only half a man, so that neither people was well without the other, nor could either be healed until the Landlord's Son <Christ> came into the country."[54]

This notion of progressive revelation reflects Lewis's belief that God disclosed Himself to man in a way best suited to His particular stage of development. For pagan culture, Divine revelation took the form of mythology. For the Hebrews, God spoke through the Law and the prophets.

But if Christianity is "myth become fact," what of the Old Testament? Lewis admitted that the Hebrews, like other ancient peoples, had their own mythology. But as they were the "Chosen People," so their mythology was the "chosen" mythology--the mythology chosen by God to be "the vehicle of the earliest sacred truths, the first step in that process which ends in the New Testament where truth has become completely historical."[55]

Where any particular story falls in this process of crystallization is a different matter. The memoirs of David's court are seen by Lewis as almost completely historical, whereas the Book of Jonah is seen "at the opposite end of the scale."[56] In fact, Lewis perceived the Old Testament narrative as progressing through a type of spiritual evolution. As he wrote in a private letter: "If you take the Bible as a whole, you see a process in which something which, on its eccentric levels (these aren't necessarily the ones that come first in the Book as now arranged) was hardly moral at all, and was in some ways not unlike the pagan religions, is gradually purged and enlightened till it becomes the religion of the great prophets, and of Our Lord Himself."[57]

In his book <u>Reflections on the Psalms</u>, Lewis confessed that he had been suspected of being a "Fundamentalist" simply because he never regarded any narrative as unhistorical solely because it included the miraculous. But Lewis denied the charge, calling for a less literalistic approach. He cited theological precedent in St. Jerome's comment that Moses described creation "after the manner of a popular poet." He also mentioned John Calvin's doubts concerning the historicity of Job. Lewis elaborated: "The <u>Book of Job</u> appears to me unhistorical because it begins about a man quite unconnected with all history or even legend, with no genealogy, living in a country of which the Bible elsewhere has hardly anything to say, because in fact the author quite obviously writes as a story-teller, not as a chronicler."[58]

Lewis did not consider the Old Testament the "Word of God" if by that is meant infallible science

"Word of God" if by that is meant infallible science or history. Instead, the Old Testament "carries" the Word of God. It should not be used as "an encyclopedia or an encyclical" but is best utilized by "steeping ourselves in its tone or temper, and so learning its overall message."[59]

Lewis was willing to accept the Genesis account of creation as derived from, though a great improvement upon, earlier Semitic stories which were pagan and mythical. But this was provided that "derived from" was interpreted to mean that the re-tellers were themselves guided by God: "When a series of such re-tellings turns a creation story which at first had almost no religious or metaphysical significance into a story which achieves the idea of true Creation and of a transcendent Creator (as Genesis does), then nothing will make me believe that some of the re-tellers, or some one of them, has not been guided by God."[60]

Although the story of creation in Genesis was seen by Lewis as mythical, that did not mean he believed it was simply "untrue." It is truer than history itself. As Lewis described his view in a private letter: "I accept the story of the Fall, and I don't see what the findings of the scientists can say either for or against it. You can't see for looking at skulls and flint implements whether Man fell or not. But the question of the Fall seems to me quite independent of the question of evolution. I don't mind whether God made Man out of earth or whether 'earth' merely means 'previous material of some sort.' If the deposits make it probable that man's physical ancestors 'evolved,' no matter. It leaves the essence of the Fall itself intact. Don't let us confuse physical development with spiritual."[61] As Lewis's friend and critic Clyde Kilby has pointed out, Lewis's frequent discussions of the Garden of Eden make it apparent that it meant "a hundred times more to him as myth than it does to most Christians as history."[62]

Lewis admitted that naivete, error, and contradiction--the human qualities of the Bible's raw materials--remain in Scripture. Scripture may even contain wickedness, as is seen in the vindictive or cursing Psalms. The Psalmist may ask God to slay his enemies, or even to "snatch up a Babylonian baby and beat his brains out against the pavement."[63]

Such passages are sinful, stated Lewis, and should not be excused, since the Hebrew's Law had plenty of teachings against vengeance and grudges. In fact, many Old Testament teachings are similar to those found in the New Testament. Lewis assumed that the modern Christian reader should read such "sinful" passages in order to suggest similar sins in his own life, even if such sins are more cleverly disguised.

God does not condone the sin revealed in the "cursing Psalms," but causes His Word to go forth even through the written account of sin and the sinner who wrote it. We must even suppose that the canonizing and work of redactors and editors was under some kind of "Divine pressure."[64]

Thus, Lewis perceived the Old Testament not as a book but as a collection of books, "so widely different in period, kind, language, and aesthetic values, that no common criticism can be passed on them."[65] Within its pages are found chronicles, poems, moral and political diatribes, romances, and myth. But all, declared Lewis, is taken into the service of God's word, though not all in the same way.

One might have expected, commented Lewis, that God would have revealed his ultimate truth in a more systematic form, something as easy to understand as the multiplication table. But even the teachings of Christ do not come to us in that way and are not a thing for the intellect alone. Instead, Christ's teachings demand a response from the whole man, demanding a new outlook and temper.

Similarly, the value of the Old Testament may in fact be dependent on what seems to be its imperfections. It may repel an overly literal use in order that one may be forced to relive the whole Jewish experience of God's gradual self-revelation, "to feel the very contentions between the Word and the human material through which it works. For here again, it is our total response that has to be elicited."[66] Lewis recognized that a chronicle of the "facts of history might leave out the essence of the Jewish experience, since history is made up not only of objective overt actions, but also of agonies, joys, and other motivations of the human soul."[67]

However, it would be a mistake to conclude that Lewis simply regarded the Old Testament as another good book: "God selected one particular people and spent several centuries hammering into their heads the sort of God He was. Those people were the Jews, and the Old Testament gives an account of the hammering process."[68]

Lewis repeatedly called the Old Testament "Holy Scripture," sharply distinguishing even between the canon and the Apocrypha. Lewis also repeatedly assured the reader that the Biblical account often turns out to be more accurate a portrayal of God's nature than our lengthy theological interpretations of it.

One commentator has pointed out that "literary inspiration" may be a useful phrase to denote Lewis's view of scripture.[69] The Old Testament is to be approached as inspired literature, with its literary elements--images, myths, symbols, and metaphors--being actual embodiments of spiritual reality or vehicles of divine inspiration.

This does not mean that the Bible can be read simply as "great literature" without recognizing its religious basis. As Lewis portrayed it: "Unless the religious claims of the Bible are again acknowledged, its literary claims will, I think, be given only 'mouth honour' and that decreasingly. For it is, through and through, a sacred book. . . . It contains good literature and bad literature. But even the good literature is so written that we can seldom disregard its sacred character. . . . It is, if you like to put it that way, not merely a sacred book, but a book so remorselessly and continuously sacred that it does not invite, it excludes or repels, the merely aesthetic approach."[70]

Much of Lewis's defense of the Old Testament stems from Christ's defense of it. Lewis defended the use of Old Testament scripture as a foreshadowing of Christianity because Christ did. Christ "clearly identified Himself with a figure often mentioned in the Scriptures: appropriated to Himself many passages where a modern scholar might see no such reference. In the predictions of His Own Passion which He had previously made to the disciples, He was obviously doing the same thing. He accepted--indeed He claimed to be--the second meaning of Scripture."[71]

Lewis also defended the "unsystematic" revelation of God found in the Old Testament. Christ's teachings were also unsystematic: "We have only reported sayings, most of them uttered in answer to questions, shaped in some degree by their context. And when we have collected them all we cannot reduce them to a system. . . . He utters maxims which, like popular proverbs, if rigorously taken, may seem to contradict one another. His teaching therefore cannot be grasped by the intellect alone, cannot be 'got up' as if it were a 'subject.'"[72] Even the poetry sections of the Old Testament are defended in part because "Our Lord, soaked in the poetic tradition of His country, delighted to use it."[73]

But what of the New Testament? In what sense is it "mythical?" Lewis drew a sharp distinction between the nature of the Gospels and other mythological literature. Lewis stated that he was too experienced in literary criticism to regard the Gospels as myths. "They had not the mythical taste. And yet the very matter which they set down in their artless, historical fashion. . . was precisely the matter of the great myths."[74]

Myths were like the Gospels in one way; histories were like it in another. But neither were simply like it. Lewis was taken with the character of Christ as depicted in the Gospels, whom he described as someone "as real, as recognizable, through all that depth of time, as Plato's Socrates, or Boswell's Johnson."[75]

For Lewis, it is the blending of the mythical and the real in a historical occurrence which gives Christianity its greatest argument for validity: "Here and here only in all time the myth must have become fact; the Word, flesh; God, Man. This is not 'a religion,' nor 'a philosophy.' It is the summing up and actuality of them all."[76]

However, if Christianity is "myth become fact," it then becomes open to historical investigation. This process of historical examination has been going on at least since the Enlightenment. The examining of the historical evidence for Christianity, referred to by Albert Schweitzer as "the quest of the historical Jesus" has had profound implications for Twentieth Century theology. Thus, any defense of the "historicity" of Christianity must in some way take the findings of this "quest" into account.

NOTES: CHAPTER TWO

[1] C. S. Lewis, They Stand Together: The Letters of C. S. Lewis to Arthur Greeves (1914-1963), ed. Walter Hooper (New York: The Macmillan Co., 1979), copyright © 1979 by the Estate of C. S. Lewis, p. 135. Used by permission.

[2] C. S. Lewis, Surprised by Joy: The Shape of My Early Life (Harcourt Brace and World, 1956), copyright © 1955 by C. S. Lewis; renewed by Arthur Owen Barfield, Executor of the Estate of C. S. Lewis, p. 173. Used by permission.

[3] Lewis, They Stand Together, pp. 135-136.

[4] Clyde S. Kilby, The Christian World of C. S. Lewis (Grand Rapids: William B. Eerdmans, 1964), p.17.

[5] Kilby, p. 17

[6] Lewis, Surprised by Joy, p. 214.

[7] Lewis, Surprised, p. 212.

[8] Lewis, Surprised, p. 213.

[9] Lewis, Surprised, p. 214.

[10] Lewis, Surprised, p. 215.

[11] C. S. Lewis, Mere Christianity (New York: Macmillan paperback, 1952), p. 119.

[12] Roger Lancelyn Green and Walter Hooper, C. S. Lewis: A Biographyggg (New York: Harcourt Brace Jovanovich, 1974), p. 44.

[13] Lewis, Mere Christianity, p. 120.

[14] Lewis, Surprised by Joy, p. 223.

[15] Lewis, Surprised, pp. 223-224.

[16] Walter Hooper, Through Joy and Beyond: A Pictorial Biography of C. S. Lewis (New York: The Macmillian Co., 1982), p. 78.

[17] Lewis, *Surprised by Joy*, p. 224.

[18] Lewis, *Surprised*, p. 228-229.

[19] Lewis, *They Stand Together*, pp. 330-331.

[20] Green and Hooper, *C. S. Lewis: A Biography*, p. 106.

[21] Lewis, *They Stand Together*, p. 425.

[22] Lewis, *They Stand Together*, p. 427-428.

[23] Lewis, *Surprised by Joy*, p. 237.

[24] Lewis, *They Stand Together*, p. 426.

[25] Humphrey Carpenter, *The Inklings: C. S. Lewis, J. R. R. Tolkien, Charles Williams and their Friends* (Boston: Houghton Mifflin, 1978), p. 223.

[26] Carpenter, p. 223.

[27] Carpenter, p. 223.

[28] C. S. Lewis, "Horrid Red Things," in his *God in the Dock: Essays on Theology and Ethics*, ed. Walter Hooper (Grand Rapids: Willam B. Eerdmans, 1970), p. 69.

[29] C. S. Lewis, *The Pilgrim's Regress: An Allegorical Apology for Christianity, Reason, and Romanticism*, 2nd ed. (Grand Rapids: William B. Eerdmans, 1958), p. 171.

[30] Carpenter, *The Inklings*, p. 43.

[31] Carpenter, p. 43.

[32] Lewis, *They Stand Together*, pp. 427-428.

[33] Christensen, Michael J., *C. S. Lewis on Scripture: His Thoughts on the Nature of Biblical Inspiration, the Role of Revelation and the Question of Inerrancy* (Waco, Texas: Word Books, 1979), p. 61.

[34] C. S. Lewis, *An Experiment in Criticism* (Cambridge: Cambridge University Press, 1966), p. 41.

[35] Lewis, *Experiment*, p. 44.

[36] Lewis, *Experiment*, p. 56.

[37] Christensen, *C. S. Lewis on Scripture*, p. 63.

[38] Lewis, "Myth Became Fact," *God in the Dock*, p. 66.

[39] Lewis, *God in the Dock* p. 66.

[40] Christensen, *C. S. Lewis on Scripture*, p. 64.

[41] C. S. Lewis, ed., *George MacDonald: An Anthology*, (New York: The Macmillan Co., 1947), p. xxviii.

[42] Lewis, *Experiment in Criticism*, p. 45.

[43] Lewis, "Myth Became Fact," *God in the Dock*, p. 66.

[44] C. S. Lewis, *Miracles: A Preliminary Study with Revision of Chapter III* (New York: Macmillan paperback, 1978), p. 134.

[45] C. S. Lewis, *Reflections on the Psalms*, (Harcourt Brace and World, 1958), p. 107.

[46] C. S. Lewis, *The Four Loves*, (Harcourt Brace and World, 1960) p. 175.

[47] Lewis, *Miracles*, p. 74.

[48] Lewis, *Miracles*, p. 74.

[49] Lewis, *The Pilgrim's Regress*, p. 152.

[50] C. S. Lewis, "Is Theology Poetry?," in his *The Weight of Glory and Other Addresses: Revised and Expanded* ed. Walter Hooper (New York: Macmillan paperback, 1980), pp. 83-84.

[51] Lewis, *Miracles*, p. 115.

[52] Lewis, *Reflections on the Psalms*, pp. 106-107.

[53] Lewis, *An Experiment in Criticism*, p. 52.

[54] Lewis, *The Pilgrim's Regress*, p. 154.

[55] Lewis, *Miracles*, p. 134.

[56] Lewis, *Miracles*, p. 134.

[57] "To a Lady," February 2, 1955, *Letters of C. S. Lewis*, pp. 262-263.

[58] Lewis, *Reflections on the Psalms*, p. 110.

[59] Lewis, *Psalms*, p.112.

[60] Lewis, *Psalms*, p. 111.

[61] Richard L. Purtill, *C. S. Lewis's Case for the Christian Faith* (New York: Harper and Row, 1981), p.58.

[62] Kilby, *The Christian World of C. S. Lewis*, p. 160.

[63] Lewis, *Reflections on the Psalms*, p. 21.

[64] Lewis, *Psalms*, p. 111.

[65] C. S. Lewis, "The Literary Impact of the Authorised Version," in his *Selected Literary Essays*, ed. Walter Hooper, (Cambridge University Press, 1969), p. 126.

[66] Lewis, *Reflections on the Psalms*, p. 114.

[67] Kilby, *The Christian World of C. S. Lewis*, p. 154.

[68] Lewis, *Mere Christianity*, p. 54.

[69] Christensen, *C. S. Lewis on Scripture*, p. 77.

[70] Lewis, "The Literary Impact of the Authorised Version," *Selected Literary Essays*, p. 144.

[71] Lewis, *Reflections on the Psalms*, p. 118.

[72] Lewis, *Psalms*, pp. 112-113.

[73] Lewis, *Psalms*, p. 5.

[74] Lewis, *Surprised by Joy*, p. 236.

[75] Lewis, *Surprised*, p. 236.

[76] Lewis, *Surprised*, p. 236.

CHAPTER THREE

C. S. LEWIS AND NEW TESTAMENT SCHOLARSHIP

C. S. Lewis wrote a warning in the Epilogue of his book <u>Miracles: A Preliminary Study</u> concerning modern Biblical scholarship. He stated: "When you turn from the New Testament to modern scholars, remember that you go among them as a sheep among wolves. Naturalistic assumptions, beggings of the question. . . will meet you on every side."[1] Lewis's attitude to contemporary scholarship was in part shaped by his belief in the weakening effect this scholarship had on Christian faith. As Lewis perceived it, "The undermining of the old orthodoxy has been mainly the work of divines engaged in New Testament criticism."[2]

One of Lewis's major criticisms of New Testament scholarship involved the naturalistic assumptions of many New Testament critics, including those within the Church. Lewis saw this partly as a result of the modern world view seeping into church theology: "This does not mean (as I was once tempted to suspect) that these clergymen are disguised apostates who deliberately exploit the position and the livelihood given them by the Christian Church to undermine Christianity. It comes partly from what we may call a 'hangover.' We all have Naturalism in our bones and even conversion does not at once work the infection out of our system."[3]

Although Lewis did not deal in detail with the findings of modern New Testament research, he did critically analyze their general approach and methods. This effort was important, Lewis felt, because the historical reality of the New Testament story was seen by him as the indispensable basis of the Christian faith. Lewis was suspicious of modern New Testament scholarship's tendencies to reject the elements of the Christian story that most clearly pointed to its nature as "myth become fact": the Divinity of Jesus, the concept of the Kingdom of God, the miraculous, and the historical validity of the Gospel record. We will examine each of these areas, analyzing not only the conclusions of various New Testament scholars but Lewis's reactions to them as well.

Jesus's Divinity

The questioning of Jesus's Divine nature has always been a challenge offered by non-believers of the Christian faith. However, the first serious challenge in the West to the belief in Jesus as the Messiah came in the late Seventeenth and early Eighteenth Century with the Enlightenment and its belief in natural law and suspicion of the supernatural.

In Germany, Hermann Samuel Reimarus (1694-1768) began a systematic criticism of the story of Jesus. Reimarus challenged the integrity of the disciples, declaring that Jesus had preached a this-worldly kingdom along the political lines of Jewish messianic expectations. As Reimarus saw it: "We are justified in drawing an absolute distinction between the teaching of the Apostles in their writings and what Jesus Himself in his own lifetime proclaimed and taught."[4] According to Reimarus, Jesus had no intention of founding a new religion. Although Jesus believed in a coming Kingdom of God, said Reimarus, he saw it as most Jews of his day did, as a reestablished independent Jewish national state.

Nevertheless, said Reimarus, after Jesus's death his disciples conjured up the vision of a "Second Coming of the Messiah," guaranteed by a resurrection they invented after stealing Jesus's body. As a result of this action, they got rid of the difficulty of his death by giving it the significance of a spiritual redemption.

In spite of the fact that Reimarus read into the text things that were not there, such as the national-political character of the Kingdom of God and the fraudulence of the disciples, Reimarus did raise the crucial question of the relationship of Jesus's own views to those of the early Christian Church.

Reimarus's presupposition of Jesus's lack of Divine pretensions was carried further by the Biblical scholar Wilhelm Wrede (1859-1906). Wrede attempted to demonstrate that Mark was much more of a theological rather than a historical source in his work: Das

Messiasgeheimnis in den Evangelien <The Messianic Secret in the Gospels> published in 1901. According to Wrede, the narratives of Mark are permeated with the theological conception of the "Messianic Secret" which Wrede felt was of post-Easter origin. For Wrede the Messianic Secret was rooted in the fact that Jesus was not recognized as Messiah by the disciples, nor by anyone, before the resurrection.

Following Wrede's conclusions, Rudolf Bultmann, perhaps the most influential Twentieth Century New Testament critic, summarized the conclusions of modern scholarship concerning Jesus's self-concept: "We can now know almost nothing concerning the life and personality of Jesus."[5] We can know something of his teaching, which Bultmann saw as primarily eschatological in character and as an appeal for decision before the approaching end.

Bultmann found the historical person of Jesus inaccessible and also denied that He ever claimed to be the Messiah. "The historical person of Jesus was very soon turned into a myth in primitive Christianity," declared Bultmann. "It is now impossible to get behind this myth to the historical facts of the matter."[6] Bultmann further declared that "the personality of Jesus has no importance for the kerygma (Greek for proclamation) either of Paul or of John. . . . Indeed the tradition of the earliest Church did not even unconsciously preserve a picture of his personality. Every attempt to reconstruct one remains a play of the subjective imagination."[7]

Lewis was highly suspicious of this effort to make a distinction between the historical Jesus and the Biblical Christ. For Lewis, the Gospels say what they say and cannot be added to or subtracted from. But Lewis was also stunned by Bultmann's claim that the personality of Jesus had no importance for the kerygma. What bothered Lewis was Bultmann's belief that the Gospel record itself provides no clues to the personality of Jesus. Lewis remarked: "If anything whatever is common to all believers, and even to many unbelievers, it is the sense that in the Gospels they have met a personality."[8] Lewis pointed out that there are many historical figures of which we do not have any "personal" knowledge, such as Alexander the Great, Attila the Hun, or William of Orange. On the other hand there are literary figures who make no claim to historical reality whom we still know as "real people." In this category he mentioned Falstaff, Uncle Toby, or Mr. Pickwick.

But, claimed Lewis, there are only three characters who can claim both a literary *and* a historical reality. They are Plato's Socrates, the Jesus of the Gospels, and Boswell's Johnson. Of course, historians have recognized that historical and literary reality do not necessarily have a direct connection. Scholars have been as puzzled in their search for the "historical" Socrates embedded in Plato's dialogues as New Testament scholars have been in their search for the historical Jesus. Also, some literary critics have implied that Boswell's Johnson may be as much a product of Boswell's genius as of Johnson's personality. But, putting aside the historical question, what shocked Lewis about Bultmann's view was that Bultmann perceived no clear personality in the Gospel record at all.

Lewis felt that the portrait of Jesus in the Gospels is not only concise but consistent in all four Gospel accounts. In the Jesus of the Gospels, Lewis found a combination of peasant shrewdness, intolerable severity, and "irresistible" tenderness. According to Lewis, "So strong is the flavour of the personality that, even while He says things which, on any other assumption than that of Divine Incarnation in the fullest sense, would be appallingly arrogant, yet we--and many unbelievers too--accept Him at His own valuation when He says 'I am meek and lowly of heart.' Even those passages in the New Testament which superficially, and in intention, are most concerned with the Divine, and least with the Human Nature, bring us face to face with the personality."[9]

The force of this personality, not the creativity of the Gospel authors, is what shaped the early church. When the claim is made by a New Testament scholar that Jesus's persona resulted from "that significance which the early church found that it was impelled to attribute to its Master" Lewis declared that the statement "hits us in the face." The early church was not impelled to create a personality for Jesus, said Lewis, but it was impelled *by* that personality to create a church. As Lewis dryly concluded: "I begin to fear that by 'personality' Dr. Bultmann means what I should call impersonality: what you'd get in a D. N. B. article or an obituary or a Victorian Life and Letters of Yeshua Bar Yosef in three volumes with photographs."[10] For Lewis not only is Jesus's personality clearly portrayed in the Gospels, but his personality is inseparable from his Divinity.

Another way scholars have dealt with the issue of Jesus's Divinity has been to down play its significance and to stress instead the role of Jesus as religious teacher. The classical example of this approach is the work of Adolf von Harnack (1851-1930), whose popular lectures, published as What is Christianity? (1900), were quickly translated into English and widely read in England and America. The problem with Harnack (and others like him) is that he had his own preconceptions of what was the essence of Jesus's message and what was superfluous. Harnack saw Jesus as a religious teacher and rejected Jesus's apocalypticism as "a miserabilism which clings to the expectation of a miraculous interference on God's part, and in the meantime, as it were, wallows in wretchedness."[11]

The true essential message of Jesus, for Harnack, centered on God as father and men as brothers. As Harnack stated: "The Gospel in the Gospel is something so simple, something that speaks to us with so much power that it cannot easily be mistaken."[12]

Harnack declared that his approach was an attempt to distinguish "what is permanent from what is fleeting, what is rudimentary from what is merely historical."[13] Of course, the problem with removing what is "merely historical" is that instead of gathering a picture of Jesus's actual teachings, one gets a projection of Harnack's own value judgments, hopes, and ideals.

Unlike Harnack, Lewis felt it was the Gospels' focus on Jesus's Divinity that was necessary in any attempt to understand Jesus as a religious teacher. Lewis was impressed by the fact that a man like Jesus appeared, claiming divinity among the very people who would most likely reject those claims. As Lewis portrayed it: "Among Pantheists, like the Indian, anyone might say that he was a part of God, or one with God: there would be nothing very odd about it. But this man, since He was a Jew, could not mean that kind of God. God, in their language, meant the Being outside the world Who made it and was infinitely different from anything else. And when you have grasped that, you will see that what this man said was, quite simply, the most shocking thing that has ever been uttered by human lips."[14]

Lewis pointed out that the claims of Jesus are quite different from those of other religious teachers and founders: "Others say, 'This is the truth about the Universe. This is the way you ought to go,' but He says, 'I am the Truth, and the Way, and the Life.' He says 'No man can reach absolute reality, except through Me. . . . I am Re-birth, I am Life. Eat Me, drink Me, I am your Food. And finally, do not be afraid, I have overcome the whole Universe.'"[15]

It is these claims of Jesus that made Lewis impatient with those who tried to maintain the validity of Jesus's moral teachings while rejecting his Divine Nature. Lewis had very little patience with those who claimed "I'm ready to accept Jesus as a great moral teacher, but I don't accept His claim to be God." As Lewis characterized it in one of his most famous remarks on the nature of Christ: "A man who was merely a man and said the sort of things Jesus said would not be a great moral teacher. He would either be a lunatic--on a level with the man who says he is a poached egg--or else he would be the Devil of Hell. You must make your choice. Either this man was, and is, the Son of God: or else a madman or something worse. You can shut Him up for a fool, you can spit at Him and kill Him as a demon; or you can fall at His feet and call Him Lord and God. But let us not come with any patronizing nonsense about His being a great human teacher. He has not left that open to us. He did not intend to."[16]

Although Lewis's prose here is highly moving, there is a third alternative which Lewis did not address. In the Synoptic Gospels Jesus often uses the term "Son of Man." Bultmann and others have acknowledged the possibility that when Jesus originally referred to the Son of Man he was not speaking of Himself but of a supernatural figure found in late Jewish apocalypticism. This "Son of Man" was associated with the final cataclysmic end of the world and was to come with the clouds of heaven to be given everlasting dominion over all people (ex: Dan 7:13f).

Thus, in the Son of Man sayings, Jesus may have originally been preaching the coming of a Savior other than Himself (ex: Mark 8:38, 14:62). Although there is still disagreement among New Testament scholars over the "Son of Man" sayings, Lewis seems to have been totally unaware of the controversy.

Still, Lewis's criticisms of the attempt to re-create a "historical Jesus" as distinct from the Biblical Christ are effective, especially in light of the fact that there has been substantial disagreement over who this "historical Jesus" actually was. From Harnack's religious philosopher to Liberation Theology's Marxist revolutionary, various writers have attempted to get behind the New Testament record to discover the real Jesus. Lewis commented on the futility of this effort in his book <u>The Screwtape Letters</u>. These comments are from a diabolical point of view, as Screwtape comments to his nephew Wormwood on the advantages of the search for a "historical" Jesus for their infernal side:

> In the last generation we promoted the construction of such a "historical" Jesus on liberal and humanitarian lines; we are now putting forward a new "historical Jesus" on Marxian, catastrophic, and revolutionary lines. The advantages of these constructions, which we intend to change every thirty years or so, are manifold. In the first place they all tend to direct men's devotion to something which does not exist, for each "historical Jesus" is unhistorical. . . . In the second place, all such constructions place the importance of their "historical Jesus" in some peculiar theory He is supposed to have promulgated. He has to be a "great man" in the modern sense. . . a crank vending a panacea . . . . Our third aim is . . . to destroy the devotional life. For the real presence of the Enemy . . . we substitute a merely probable, remote, shadowy, and uncouth figure, one who spoke a strange language and died a long time ago. . . . And fourthly, besides being unhistorical in the Jesus it depicts, religion of this kind is false to history in another sense. . . . The earliest converts were converted by a

single historical fact (the Resurrection) and a single theological doctrine (the Redemption). . . . The "Gospels" come later.[17]

As can be seen in the above passage, Lewis was suspicious of the "historical Jesus" movement because he suspected it of distorting the historical documents in order to create a picture of the "historical" Jesus that is distinct from the Gospel record. Since this image is not found in the Gospel records themselves, it varies with the times. Thus, in a thirty year period Lewis had seen the shift in the portrayal of Jesus from the liberal philosopher to the Marxist revolutionary. Further, he suspected the historical Jesus movement of placing primary emphasis on Jesus's peculiar religious beliefs and theories rather than on Jesus as Incarnate God. As a result, the modern study of Jesus has created an image of a remote and alien figure unworthy of worship.

Lewis believed that one cannot study the Gospel record successfully except from the standpoint of faith, since the Gospels were intended for Christian converts and not for the conversion of unbelievers. It was the <u>kerygma</u>, declared Lewis, which formed the center point of early Christian faith. All understanding of the Gospel record stems from the existential recognition of the fact of sin and the need for that sin to be atoned for by the death and resurrection of Christ. Without the basic presupposition of these elements, implied Lewis, the Gospel record itself becomes unintelligible. Instead of the mythic power of an Incarnate God we are left with the portrait of a man who dispenses various religious truisms.

It was the overwhelming power of the picture of Jesus as Incarnate God, of "myth become fact" that most affected Lewis's perceptions of the Gospels. That image of Jesus as God-man was the central point of Christianity for Lewis. When various New Testament critics questioned that aspect of the Christian message, Lewis felt he had to reject their findings or reject what gave Christianity its mythic power. Lewis sensed a numinous presence in, with, and under the objective data that many New Testament scholars seemed to miss.

The Kingdom of God

The validity of Jesus's claim to Divinity is closely tied to the validity of his message. A large part of this message deals with the concept of the Kingdom of God. This is particularly true in the Synoptic Gospels with the Kingdom of God being referred to over one hundred times as compared to only thirty-four references in the rest of the New Testament.

Although the Kingdom of God is said to be present in some sense in Jesus's mission and message, there is also a strong futuristic emphasis. Jesus declared the Kingdom to be future, though imminent. For example, after the confession of Peter at Caesarea Philippi, Jesus instructed the disciples, "Truly, I say to you, there are some standing here who will not taste death before they see the Kingdom of God come with power (Mark 9:1, Matthew 16:28, Luke 9:27)." Similarly, the Apocalyptic Discourse (Mark 13, Matthew 24, Luke 21) speaks several times of the tribulations of the end time, the coming of the judgment, and the ushering in of the rule of God.

Much of modern Biblical scholarship's awareness of the importance of the Kingdom of God in Jesus's message is due to the insights of Albert Schweitzer (1875-1965). In his book <u>The Quest of the Historical Jesus</u> (1906), Schweitzer declared that an apocalyptic emphasis was at the very core of Jesus's teachings. Schweitzer showed how fallacious Harnack's approach was to the historical figure of Jesus. According to Schweitzer, in attempting to create a "Jesus for today," Harnack and others were turning Jesus into an idealist, a rationalist, a socialist, or a romanticist, depending on the researcher's own preconceptions. For Schweitzer, the apocalyptic element was not the outer husk of Jesus's teaching but its very center. By ignoring that apocalyptic element, Schweitzer felt one got a totally distorted picture of Jesus's own conception of his mission.

Schweitzer developed his own view of Jesus, portraying Him as a man whose whole life was focused on God's imminent cataclysmic overthrow of world history. That very factor in Jesus's teaching, which liberals dismissed as "dogmatic," unhistorical and unimportant, Schweitzer emphasized as the genuinely historical factor of Jesus's ministry.

According to Schweitzer, the heart of Jesus's message was that God would suddenly put an end to the world and history and would bring in a new world in the very near future. When the disciples returned from their tour of the cities of Israel and still the new world had not arrived, Schweitzer believed that Jesus felt constrained to force the hand of God. Schweitzer believed that Jesus purposely gave His life to set the eschatological process in motion.

As Schweitzer explained: "Jesus, in the knowledge that He is the coming Son of Man, lays hold of the wheel of the world to set it moving on that last revolution which is to bring all ordinary history to a close. It refuses to turn, and He throws Himself upon it. Then it does turn; and crushes Him. . . . The wheel rolls onward, and the mangled body of the one immeasurably great Man, who was strong enough to think of Himself as the spiritual ruler of mankind and to bend history to His purpose is hanging upon it still. That is His victory and His reign."[18]

Schweitzer's work had a devastating effect on the idealistic approach to Jesus's teachings, placing Jesus instead in the First Century world of Jewish apocalyptic. Schweitzer concluded that this distant Jesus can come to us now, not as an easily understood "modern," but only as "One unknown."

Other scholars, although taking a less radical view, also saw Jesus as predicting an imminent end-time. Later, in the light of the Easter experience, the early church is said by some scholars to have identified the coming of the Kingdom of God with the return of Christ to judge the world. As it says in the Book of Acts: "Men of Galilee, why do you stand looking into heaven? This Jesus who was taken up from you into heaven, will come in the same way as you saw him go into heaven (Acts 1:11)." Gradually, as the predictions of the imminent return remained unfulfilled, the church is seen as decreasing its emphasis on the "second coming," explaining the fewer references to that event in the Gospel of John and the later epistles.

Lewis, in defending the accuracy of the New

Testament record of Jesus's message, had to deal both with the predictions of the end-time and their seeming inaccuracy. Lewis himself acknowledged that many well-meaning Christians have found the doctrine of the Second Coming meaningless and outdated. Sounding a bit like Adolf von Harnack, Lewis paraphrased their argument as follows: "Every great man is partly of his own age and partly for all time. What matters in his work is always that which transcends his age, not that which he shared with a thousand forgotten contemporaries. We value Shakespeare for the glory of his language and his knowledge of the human heart, which were his own; not for his belief in witches or the divine right of kings, or his failure to take a daily bath. So with Jesus. His belief in a speedy and catastrophic end to history belongs to him not as a great teacher, but as a first-century Palestinian peasant. It was one of his inevitable limitations, best forgotten. We must concentrate on what distinguished him from other first-century Palestinian peasants, on his moral and social teaching."[19]

Although Lewis stated the argument against eschatology well, he disagreed with it. According to Lewis, the argument against the reality of the Second Coming seems to beg the question. As Lewis analyzed it: "When we propose to ignore in a great man's teaching those doctrines which it has in common with the thought of his age, we seem to be assuming that the thought of his age was erroneous. When we select for serious consideration those doctrines which 'transcend' the thought of his own age and are 'for all time,' we are assuming that the thought of our age is correct. . . . No one would reject Christ's apocalyptic on the ground that apocalyptic was common in first century Palestine unless he had already decided that the thought of first-century Palestine was in that respect mistaken."[20]

But what about Jesus's own prediction of the imminence of the Kingdom of God? He predicted that "there are some standing here who will not taste death before they see the Kingdom of God come with power (Mark 9:1)"? Lewis admitted that this is "the most embarrassing verse in the Bible."[21] But Lewis pointed out that in his discussion of the end time Jesus also made the statement: "But of that day or that hour no one knows, not even the angels in heaven, nor the

Son, but only the Father (Mark 13:32)."

Interestingly enough, Lewis tried to turn an exhibition of error and a confession of ignorance into a defense of the validity of the Gospel record. As Lewis saw it: "This passage (Mark 13:30-32) and the cry 'Why hast thou forsaken me?' (Mark 15:34) together make up the strongest proof that the New Testament is historically reliable. The evangelists have the first great characteristic of honest witnesses: they mention facts which are at first sight damaging to their main contention."[22] Of course, depending on the dating of the Gospel record, the Gospel writers might still have been living in the hope that Jesus's prophecy would soon be fulfilled.

Lewis goes on to see Jesus's confession of ignorance as an indication of the nature of the Incarnation. For Jesus to be fully human, stated Lewis, he would have to suffer some of the limitations of a human being, including ignorance of the future. As Lewis described it: "It would be difficult, and, to me, repellent, to suppose that Jesus never asked a genuine question, that is, a question to which he did know the answer. That would make of his humanity something so unlike ours as scarcely to deserve the name. I find it easier to believe that when he said 'Who touched me?' (Luke 7:45) he really wanted to know."[23]

For Lewis, Jesus's teaching on the subject of the Second Coming consisted of three propositions: (1) that he will certainly return, (2) that we cannot possibly find out when, (3) therefore, we must always be ready for him. Lewis concluded that the doctrine of the Second Coming is uncongenial to modern man because it is uncongenial to the whole evolutionary or developmental character of modern thought. We have been taught to think of the world as something that grows slowly towards perfection, that "progresses" or "evolves." Christian apocalyptic thought, on the other hand, foretells a sudden, violent end, imposed from without.

When the Biblical scholar Rudolf Bultmann stated in reference to Jesus's predictions of the end time: "History did not come to an end, and, as every schoolboy knows, it will continue to run its course,"[24] he was, from Lewis's point of view, assuming "the modern myth of evolutionism or developmentalism or progress in general."[25]

For Lewis, the value of the doctrine of the Second Coming was that it challenged the Zeitgeist of the current age, the belief that the world is slowly ripening to perfection. This view, stated Lewis, is a myth, not a generalization from experience. He concluded: "The doctrine of the Second Coming then, is not to be rejected because it conflicts with our favorite modern mythology. It is for that very reason, to be the more valued and made more frequently the subject of meditation."[26]

According to Lewis, this doctrine of the Second Coming forces the Christian to evaluate all of his actions in light of the final judgement. It also allows him to realize that not only individuals are transitory; empires and civilizations are transitory as well. Whereas Bultmann tended to speak of the "eschatological myth" as illuminating on the individual existential level, Lewis saw it extending to the societal level.

This realization, Lewis felt, may correct the tendency of some modernistic theologians and ideologues to speak as though duties to posterity were the only duties they had. As Lewis argued: "I can imagine no man who will look with more horror on the End than a conscientious revolutionary who has, in a sense sincerely, been justifying cruelties and injustices inflicted on millions of his contemporaries by the benefits which he hopes to confer on future generations: generations who, as one terrible moment now reveals to him, were never going to exist. Then he will see the massacres, the faked trials, the deportations, to be all ineffaceably real, an essential part, his part, in the drama that has just ended: while the future Utopia had never been anything but a fantasy."[27]

Lewis saw in the effort to undermine Jesus's concept of the Kingdom of God as false and outdated, an attempt not to correct the Gospel record but to replace the Christian mythic world view with a world view more congenial to modern sensibilities. Thus, this effort was not a correction of the Gospel record, but a replacement of one mythology with another. It was an attempt Lewis felt compelled to reject.

The Miraculous

Lewis found that much New Testament scholarship rejected the miraculous as legendary without establishing a clear basis for this rejection. With the rejection of the miraculous, the mythic elements of the Christian story are also lost. The modern world view is uncongenial to the idea of miraculous interferences with nature, but Lewis believed that this suspicion of miracles reflected prejudice rather than reasoned thought.

For example, Bultmann wrote: "It is impossible to use electric light and the wireless and to avail ourselves of modern medical and surgical discoveries and at the same time to believe in the New Testament world of demons and spirits."[28] This statement may reflect the fact that the modern mind has been shaped by the picture of a mechanical universe operating according to uniform and unvarying laws rather than the fact that new scientific and philosophical discoveries have rendered the belief in the miraculous untenable. In other words, what we learn from experience depends on the philosophy we bring to it.

Lewis dealt at greatest length with the problem of the miraculous in his book <u>Miracles: A Preliminary Study</u>. Lewis made it clear that he was not a historian and that he did not intend to examine the historical evidence for specific miracles.[29] It is up to the historian to study the evidence for any particular miracle. Lewis's main concern was to establish the <u>possibility</u> of miracles in the face of modern skepticism. He defined a miracle as "an interference with Nature by supernatural power,"[30] which of course supposes the existence of a Supernature as well as a Nature.

In Lewis's treatment of the Christian miracle tradition, he concluded that of all the religions of the world, Christianity is the most reliant on the miraculous if its claims are to be considered valid. According to Lewis, "All the essentials of Hinduism would, I think, remain unimpaired if you subtracted the miraculous, and the same is almost true of

Mohammedanism. But you cannot do that with Christianity. It is precisely the story of a great Miracle. A naturalistic Christianity leaves out all that is specifically Christian."[31] It also loses the mythic power of the Christian story. Those who attempt to create a naturalistic Christianity based solely on Jesus's ethics or compassion for the outcast are for Lewis undercutting the very ground on which those ethics and compassion are based.

One argument against the validity of the miraculous in the New Testament is the limited scientific world-view of the New Testament writers. Not understanding the nature of scientific law, the Gospel writers ascribed the miraculous to otherwise unexplainable events. But modern man knows differently.

Lewis labeled the above attitude "chronological snobbery." Joseph, he pointed out, was fully as aware as any modern obstetrician that a virgin birth is contrary to nature. That is why at first Joseph decided to repudiate Mary. It was only after he was convinced that a miracle had occurred that he married her. Lewis summed up: "If there ever were men who did not know the laws of nature at all, they would have no idea of a miracle and feel no particular interest in one if it were performed before them. . . Belief in miracles, far from depending on an ignorance of the laws of nature, is only possible in so far as those laws are known."[32]

However, Lewis did not see miracles as a "violation" of the laws of nature. Instead, "The divine art of miracles is not an art of suspending the pattern to which events conform but of feeding new events into that pattern."[33] A miracle is an act of God when He introduces a new situation into Nature. The virgin pregnancy of Mary is the result of a miracle, but her delivery represents Nature responding to the miracle and assimilating it into normal cause-and-effect operation. Miracles do not destroy the normal course of nature. They merely interrupt it. As Lewis critic Chad Walsh described it: "If miracles do actually occur, they represent not God's arbitrary caprice, but rather a law above the law of Nature. God is like a poet who knows when to suspend the metrical rules that are ordinarily proper."[34]

If miracles are possible, Lewis saw the criterion

for any particular miracle in its "fitness". In other words, does it seem the kind of deed that would be performed by the God of Reason and Morality? Lewis did not reject "a priori" the claim that pagans also had their miracles. "I am in no way committed," Lewis declared, "to the assertion that God has never worked miracles through and for Pagans or never permitted created supernatural beings to do so."[35] What troubled Lewis about many of the pagan "miracle stories" was their lack of fitness in terms of rationality or moral sense. As Lewis argued: "The immoral, and sometimes almost idiotic interferences attributed to gods in Pagan stories, even if they had a trace of historical evidence, could be accepted only on the condition of our accepting a wholly meaningless universe."[36]

Lewis contrasted these puzzling, sometimes troubling, pagan "miracles" with what he termed the "Grand Miracle," the Incarnation of Christ. Lewis admitted that there were Christian legends just as much as there were heathen legends. But all the "well-established" miracles of the Christian faith either prepared for, or exhibited, or resulted from the Grand Miracle, the Incarnation.

In a recognition of the mythic power of the Christian narrative, Lewis argued that the descent of God to earth and His subsequent ascent correspond to the archetypal patterns of Nature itself. Nature belittles itself into tiny, hard seeds and these are buried; out of this death new life comes. The pattern one finds in nature was first in God. Christ is the fulfillment of the pagan stories of a corn-God like Adonis or Osiris. But Christ is not a legendary figure. He is a man who lived at a particular time and in a particular place, under a particular Roman governor.

Lewis pointed out that the New Testament writers spoke as if Christ's achievement in rising from the dead was the first event of its kind "in the whole history of the universe."[37] Lewis continued: "He has met, fought, and beaten the King of Death. Everything is different because He has done so. This is the beginning of the New Creation: a new chapter in cosmic history has opened."[38]

Lewis concluded that the whole concept of New Creation involves the belief that the estrangement between humankind and God and between humankind and nature will be healed. Lewis affirmed not only the historicity of the resurrection but of the ascension as well. He admitted that Luke's description of the ascension may reflect an outmoded world view, placing Christ on a chair in the sky next to God's throne. But Lewis found profound meaning in this imagery: "The archaic type of thought which could not clearly distinguish spiritual Heaven from the sky is from our point of view a confused type of thought. But it also resembles and anticipates a type of thought that will one day be true. That archaic sort of thinking will become simply the correct sort when Nature and Spirit are fully harmonized--when Spirit rides Nature so perfectly that the two together make rather a "Centaur" than a mounted knight. . . . Those who attain the glorious resurrection will see the dry bones clothed again with flesh, the fact and the myth re-married, the literal and the metaphorical rushing together."[39]

Thus, Lewis confirmed his deep-seated conviction that the miraculous is an indispensable element in the Christian faith. As he was to write elsewhere, "We may not believe in a flat earth and a sky-palace. But we must insist from the beginning that we believe, as firmly as any savage or theosophist, in a spirit-world which can, and does, invade the natural or phenomenal universe."[40]

The Historical Validity of the Gospels

Lewis felt that his belief in Christianity as "myth become fact" depended in part on the validity of the source materials about Christianity and its founder. If those source materials were shown to be questionable, so then would be the factual nature of Christianity's beginnings. This area of the historical accuracy of the Gospels was to be a major source of contention between Lewis and modern New Testament scholars.

For much of Western History, the question of the accuracy of the Gospels did not arise. So long as the Gospels were considered to be sacred books containing revealed truth, any seeming discrepancy was only an apparent difficulty. Martin Luther had declared "The Gospels follow no order in recording the acts and miracles of Jesus, and the matter is not, after all, of much importance. If a difficulty arises in regard to the Holy Scripture and we cannot solve it, we must just let it alone."[41]

However, Protestant reformers like Luther focused renewed attention on the Scriptures as the sole arbiter of Christian faith and life and created a climate of general interest in the New Testament. The Reformers also called into question the supreme place of the Roman Catholic Church's ecclesiastical authorities in interpreting the Scriptures, and it was not such a great step from that position to a critical examination of the New Testament itself.[42]

John Locke (1632-1704) published a book in 1695 entitled <u>The Reasonableness of Christianity as Delivered in Scriptures</u>. In it Locke tried to reconcile Christianity with "reason." Locke drew parallels between Christ and Plato, pointing out that although Plato's rationality taught him that there was only one God, Plato still went along with the popular polytheism of his day. So too, Christ may have gone along with the popular misconceptions of his followers in order to bring them to a deeper spiritual truth.[43]

Another writer, Matthew Tindal (1653-1733) dealt with the question of special revelation in his book <u>Christianity as Old as the Creation; Or, The Gospel, A Republication of the Religion of Nature</u> (1730). Tindal maintained that what was true in Christianity was not peculiar to it, and what was peculiar to it was not to be regarded as true. The writings of Locke and Tindal helped create an atmosphere of free thinking in which a new examination of the Gospel records themselves could take place.

By the early part of the Nineteenth Century there was an attempt to develop a purely historical approach to the Gospels. Heinrich Julius Holtzmann (1832-1910) sought to answer the question "What can be known historically about the origins of Christianity in general and about the life of Jesus in particular?" In his work, <u>The Synoptic Gospels: Their Origin and Historical Character</u> (1863), Holtzmann convincingly argued the hypothesis that Mark was the first written Gospel and was used as a source by both Luke and Matthew. Holtzmann went on to show that Matthew and Luke had used a common "sayings" source in their Gospels called "Q" (from the German word Quelle--source). This source explained parallel passages in Matthew and Luke, such as the Sermon on the Mount, that had no corresponding parallels in Mark.

That Mark is the oldest of the Gospels and that Matthew and Luke have a common sayings source is still almost universally accepted among Biblical scholars today. However, Twentieth Century scholars have attempted to move behind the literary stage by analyzing, classifying, and reconstructing the history of the originally oral forms or units in which the Gospel tradition was handed down before being preserved in written form. This approach came to be known as "form criticism," from the German Formgeschichte, literally "form-history." The most influential form critic was the German scholar Rudolf Bultmann.

In 1921 Bultmann published his monumental History of the Synoptic Tradition. Bultmann attempted an exhaustive analysis of the Gospel tradition: classifying it by type, showing how it was modified in the process of oral transmission, and indicating how the evangelists brought it together in order to make it serve their own special aims.

Bultmann felt that the Gospel of Mark was of primary importance since Mark first created the literary form "Gospel", which both Matthew and Luke followed and expanded upon. But Bultmann's analysis of the Gospels led him to a profound skepticism concerning their historical value.

Bultmann held that the history of Jesus was quickly transformed into myth, but not Lewis's "myth become fact." Bultmann felt it was futile to try to get behind the myth to the facts of the historical Jesus. These facts, whatever they were originally, have undergone an "irreversible" metamorphosis into the story of a divine, pre-existent being who became incarnate and atoned by his blood for the sins of men. This central story is embellished and illustrated by all kinds of peripheral legends which tell of miracles and wonders, voices from heaven, demonic possessions, and so on. As Bultmann saw it, many of these legends belonged to the thinking of a pre-scientific age, when any unexplained event was given a supernatural cause.

Thus for example, the Gospel of Mark is useful in determining the beliefs of the early Church, but it tells us little about the historical reality on which that Church is based. As a New Testament scholar influenced by Bultmann has written, "The Gospel of Mark is the prototype which the others follow and it is a mixture of historical reminiscence, interpreted tradition, and a strange mixture of history, legend and myth."[44]

Although not all scholars agreed with Bultmann's conclusions concerning the reliability of the Gospels, his use of "form criticism" has become a major factor in shaping Twentieth Century New Testament scholarship. A more recent development is the study of individual Gospel writers to see how, through their selection, arrangement, and modification of the Gospel tradition, each has presented Jesus in such a way as to convey the Gospel writer's own distinctive understanding of Him. This approach came to be known as <u>Redaktionsgeschichte</u> or "redaction criticism."

Redaction critics claimed that there was not <u>one</u> image of Jesus in the early church but several, and that each Gospel writer felt free to adapt and shape the traditions concerning Jesus in order to serve their own community's needs and purposes. Redaction criticism did not attack the assumptions of form criticism but accepted and used them in an analysis of how the Gospel writers shaped their material.

When dealing with the results of New Testament scholarship, Lewis admitted that his expertise was as a literary critic, not a historical scholar. But it was as literary critic that he was most skeptical of New Testament research. In a talk entitled "Modern Theology and Biblical Criticism", Lewis specifically addressed the problems posed by modern Biblical studies. Lewis rejected the practice of form critics who analyzed the various fragments of the Gospels to determine their original meaning. He suspected their presuppositions determined their conclusions. For example, Lewis quoted from Bultmann's <u>Theology of the New Testament</u>, "Observe in what unassimilated fashion the prediction of the parousia (Mark 8:38) follows upon the prediction of the passion (Mark 8:31)."[45]

Lewis declared that as a literary critic, he was baffled by Bultmann's use of the word "unassimilated." Lewis continued: "Peter has confessed Jesus to be the Anointed One. That flash of glory is hardly over before the dark prophecy begins--that the Son of Man must suffer and die. Then this contrast is repeated. Peter, raised for a moment by his confession, makes his false step; the crushing rebuff 'Get thee behind me' follows. Then, across that momentary ruin which Peter (as so often) becomes, the voice of the Master, turning to the crowd, generalizes the moral. All His followers must take up the cross. This avoidance of suffering, this self-preservation, is not what life is really about. Then, more definitely still, the summons to martyrdom. You must stand to your tackling. If you disown Christ here and now, He will disown you later. Logically, emotionally, imaginatively, the sequence is perfect. Only a Bultmann could think otherwise."[46]

Lewis suspected that Bultmann's real reason for assuming that the prediction of the parousia is unassimilated was that Bultmann assumed that predictions of the parousia are older than those of the passion. Therefore, when they occur in the same passage some discrepancy must be perceptible between them. But, said Lewis, foisting this preconception on the text results in a "shocking lack of perception."[47]

In a similar vein, Lewis was highly suspicious of the form critic who tries to reconstruct an original teaching or claim of Jesus that had become rapidly misunderstood and misrepresented by Jesus's followers. Lewis recognized, as Schweitzer had before him, the immense difficulties of trying to reconstruct the world view of a time and place distant from the critic. How can we, Twentieth Century men separated by almost two thousand years, claim an understanding of the Gospel texts that the early church lacked? As Lewis saw it, "The idea that any man or writer should be opaque to those who lived in the same culture, spoke the same language, shared the same habitual imagery and unconscious assumptions, and yet be transparent to those who have none of these advantages, is in my opinion preposterous. There is an 'a priori' improbability in it which almost no argument and no evidence could counterbalance."[48]

Lewis was also highly skeptical of the attempt to "reconstruct the genesis" of the Gospel texts, that is, "what vanished documents each author used, when and where he wrote, with what purposes, under what influences--the whole Sitz im Leben of the text."[49] Part of Lewis's suspicion concerning this approach resulted from the fact that reviewers of Lewis's own work consistently failed to reconstruct the supposed genesis of his books. As Lewis described it, "Until you come to be reviewed yourself, you would never believe how little of an ordinary review is taken up by criticism in the strict sense: by evaluation, praise, or censure, of the book actually written. Most of it is taken up with imaginary histories of the process by which you wrote it."[50]

Lewis noted that critics were not only mistaken about the origins of his works but also were wrong about the real history of the writings of his friends. Not only were they wrong, they were wrong one hundred percent of the time: "You would expect that by mere chance they would hit as often as they miss. But it is my impression that they do no such thing. I can't remember a single hit."[51]

Lewis gave an example in the intended symbolism of the Ring in J. R. R. Tolkien's The Lord of the Rings. Many critics interpreted the Ring as being suggested by the atomic bomb. Lewis continued: "What could be more plausible? Here is a book published when everyone was preoccupied by that sinister invention; here in the center of the book is a weapon which it seems madness to throw away yet fatal to use. Yet in fact, the chronology of the book's composition makes the theory impossible."[52]

If a contemporary reviewer of a man's work is consistently wrong, said Lewis, how can we expect the record of New Testament critics to be better? "The superiority in judgement and diligence which you are going to attribute to the Biblical critics will have to be almost superhuman if it is to offset the fact that they are everywhere faced with customs, language, race-characteristics, class-characteristics, a religious background, habits of composition, and basic assumptions, which no scholarship will ever enable any man now alive to know as surely and intimately and instinctively as the reviewer can know mine. And for the very same reason, remember the Biblical critics, whatever reconstructions they devise, can never be proved wrong. St. Mark is dead. When they meet St. Peter there will be more pressing matters to discuss."[53]

Another important insight of form and redaction criticism is the variance of information within the Gospels themselves. Some New Testament scholars suspect that the inconsistencies in the Gospels result from the actuality that the Gospels are theological rather than historical documents. Thus Luke mentions Jesus's resurrection appearance in Jerusalem because of that city's theological significance for Luke. In contrast, the resurrection appearances in Matthew occur in Galilee and the earliest manuscripts of Mark mention no appearances at all. Similarly, Matthew mentions Jesus's family's escape to Egypt because of its parallel to the history of the Jewish people, while Luke, a Gentile, mentions only their uneventful return to Nazareth.

Lewis, in all his apologetic works, was largely silent on what some New Testament critics have called "the Synoptic problem," the apparent discrepancies found between Matthew, Mark, and Luke. Lewis's own attempts to explain obvious problems with the New Testament texts were often simplistic. He explained the inclusion of Jesus's prayer at Gethsemane by saying that Jesus probably prayed aloud, and that the disciples must have heard the opening words of the prayer before they went to sleep. Thus, they record those opening words as if they were the whole.[54]

In a similar vein, Lewis explained in the following way why St. Luke gave such an odd description of Tertullos's speech in Acts 24: "St. Luke, though an excellent narrator, was no good as a reporter. He starts off by trying to memorize, or to get down, the whole speech verbatim. And he succeeds in reproducing a certain amount of the exordium. But he is soon defeated. The whole of the rest of the speech has to be represented by a ludicrously inadequate abstract. But he doesn't tell us what has happened, and thus seems to attribute to Tertullos a performance which would have spelled professional ruin."⁵⁵ Oddly enough, Lewis seems here to be violating his own warning against attempts at reconstructing the process by which a literary work was written.

Lewis conceded in his book <u>Miracles: A Preliminary Study</u>, that the ending of the Gospel of Mark was probably not found in the earliest texts.⁵⁶ But, beyond a few acknowledgements of inconsistencies in the New Testament record, Lewis accepted that record as historically accurate. As the critic Chad Walsh described him, "It appears that Lewis believes the New Testament very much as a Fundamentalist does. The Incarnation, the Resurrection, the Ascension, Christ's miracles--these he accepts as historical facts, as definite as Caesar's invasion of Gaul. At the same time, he attributes to them a 'mythological' significance. He parts company with the Fundamentalists by granting that large parts of the Old Testament belong to a second level--not history, but truth in mythical form on the road toward becoming historical."⁵⁷

Lewis's rejection of the Old Testament as history, however, is grounded on literary, not rationalistic grounds. As he wrote to Corbin Carnell on the subject in 1953, "Where I doubt the historicity of an Old Testament narrative I never do so on the ground that the miraculous as such is incredible. Nor does it deny a unique sort of inspiration: allegory, parable, romance, and lyric might be inspired as well as chronicle."⁵⁸

One can see that Lewis assigned portions of the Old Testament to a solely mythical level while he assumed that the New Testament must almost in its entirety be both mythical <u>and</u> historical. But following Lewis's line of argument to its logical conclusion, if allegory, parable, and romance may be "Divinely" inspired as well as chronicle, perhaps the Gospels can be inspired in non-historical ways too.

Lewis not only affirmed the historical accuracy of the Synoptic tradition, he also defended the historical nature of the Gospel of John. Although the literary aspects of the Synoptic Gospels have only recently been fully appreciated, moderately conservative Gospel scholars have often assigned the Gospel of John to the level of "literary" rather than "historical" inspiration.

As C. H. Dodd, Emeritus Professor of Cambridge University, summed up John's style, "In the process of bringing out the symbolical value of the facts he has used some freedom. Like many ancient writers, he has put into the mouth of his characters speeches which, since they bear not only the stamp of his own style, but also the stamp of an environment different from that in which the recorded events took place, cannot be regarded as historical. This use of freely composed speeches to elucidate the significance of events does not in itself impugn the historical character of the narrative in the Fourth Gospel any more than in Thucydides or Tacitus. There is however good reason to suspect that in some cases and in some respects the narratives which provide the setting for such speeches may have been moulded by the ideas which they are made to illustrate."[59]

Lewis's reading of the Fourth Gospel found no problem with the "literary" nature of the writing-style: "Apart from bits of the Platonic dialogues, there are no conversations that I know of in ancient literature like the Fourth Gospel. There is nothing, even in modern literature, until about a hundred years ago when the realistic novel came into existence. In the story of the woman taken in adultery we are told Christ bent down and scribbled in the dust with His finger. Nothing comes of this. No one has ever based any doctrine on it. And the art of inventing little irrelevant details to make an imaginary scene more convincing is a purely modern art. Surely the only explanation of this passage is that the thing really happened? The author put it in simply because he had seen it?"[60]

Lewis was particularly critical of a type of Biblical scholarship that tried to remove the Fourth Gospel from the realm of history altogether. Lewis was stunned to read in Walter Lock's commentary on the Gospel of John that the Fourth Gospel was to be regarded as a "spiritual romance, a poem not a history," to be judged by the same canon as Nathan's parable, the Book of Jonah, Paradise Lost, "or more exactly Pilgrim's Progress."[61]

When Lewis turned from Pilgrim's Progress, an

obvious allegory, to the dialogues of John, such as Jesus and the Samaritan woman at the well, he concluded that "either this is reportage--though it may no doubt contain errors--pretty close up to the facts. . . or else some unknown writer in the second century. . . anticipated the whole technique of modern, novelistic, realistic narrative. If it is untrue, it must be narrative of that kind. The reader who doesn't see this has simply not learned to read."[62]

However, it is that very artistry as a literary work that makes some scholars skeptical of the historical nature of John's Gospel. Its language is often symbolic, abstract, and complicated. The Gospel's incidents are often unique, there are seeming conflicts with the Synoptic account, and Jesus's discourses center on his Divine role rather than on the coming Kingdom of God.

Still, Lewis saw John's focus on Jesus as Divine Savior as a fuller spelling out of what is already emphasized about Jesus's nature in the Synoptics. It is this focus in the Gospel of John on Jesus's Divinity that Lewis feels is necessary in any attempt to understand Jesus as religious teacher.

Conclusion

Lewis defended in his apologetic writings much of what modern world tended to ignore or reject. He defended the historicity of the Biblical record in spite of much modern Biblical scholarship, the eschatological world view in the face of modern "evolutionism," and arguments for the miraculous in defiance of a deep-seated "naturalism." Lewis did this to defend Christianity against what he saw as the onslaughts of unbelief. Many of his insights into the weaknesses of a too rigid "form critical" approach have been incorporated into the new "literary analysis" school of Scriptural study.

Still, Lewis did not ultimately come to grips with the results of New Testament research. His analysis of the Synoptic problem was simplistic, his affirmation of the Gospel of John ignored knotty historical and literary problems, and his affirmation of Jesus's Divinity failed to come to grips with the "Son of Man" debate.

There seems to have been an increasing awareness on Lewis's part that he had relied too greatly on a rational defense of Christianity and not enough on the mythical power of the Christian story itself. Eight months after the publication of the original edition of <u>Miracles</u>, Lewis was challenged in a public debate with G. E. M. Anscombe, a well known English philosopher and Catholic. At a meeting of the Socratic Club in Oxford on February 2, 1948, Miss Anscombe, in a very technical analysis, attacked Lewis's arguments in his chapter "The Cardinal Difficulty of Naturalism."

The adequacy and effectiveness of Miss Anscombe's attack is still being debated. But the effect on Lewis seemed to have alerted him to something his friends had warned him of much earlier. "Charles Williams, listening to his wartime broadcasts, had expressed serious reservations about his tendency to make Reason the primary basis for belief in God, while Tolkien was aware of Lewis's too close reliance on supposedly infallible dialectics."[63]

The encounter with Miss Anscombe did not shatter Lewis's belief in reason. He in no way repudiated his apologetic works and later revised the third chapter of <u>Miracles</u> to avoid the difficulties Miss Anscombe pointed out.

However, as Peter Schakel related, "There is a movement away from apologetics after the forties which, combined with its broadened approach to myth, suggests that Lewis has reassessed his earlier heavy reliance upon reason." [64]

Lewis once commented on the problem of being a Christian apologist. According to Lewis, an apologist who is focusing on arguments for the existence of God cannot at the same time be tasting the reality of God. Lewis stated: "I have found that nothing is more dangerous to one's own faith than the work of an apologist. No doctrine of that Faith seems to me so spectral, so unreal as one that I have just successfully defended in a public debate. . . . We apologists . . . can be saved only by falling back continually from the web of our own arguments . . . into the Reality--from Christian apologetics into Christ himself."[65]

Peter Schakel has noted that Lewis eventually came to question a strict apologetic approach to Christianity. This questioning was partly a result of the reaction to his book <u>Miracles</u> and partly the result of his inconclusive debate with Miss Anscombe.[66] Although Lewis continued to write apologetics in articles and books, Schakel discerned a shift in Lewis's writing after 1950 to another mode of writing about Christianity. As Schakel perceived it, "His turning to myth is not a rejection of his earlier mode, but an effort to go beyond it, and to offer a reader not 'knowledge' of God, but a 'taste' of Divine Reality. That effort was at least partially successful in the <u>Chronicles of Narnia</u>."[67]

As another critic, Chad Walsh, has declared, it is in Lewis's concept of myth and imagination that his real contribution to a deeper understanding of Christianity can be seen. Walsh concluded, "In him is combined the primal intuitions of a shaman. The roots of his vision lie in the unconscious mind where we are still one with the cave men painting sacred pictures on the wall. Thus Lewis, far from being an escapist, is a writer who renews our contact with the ever-present but often ignored sources of our psychic life."[68]

It is Lewis's method of recreating imaginatively the world of the New Testament in both fiction and prose, bringing to life the power of myth, to which we will now turn.

NOTES: CHAPTER THREE

[1] C. S. Lewis, Miracles: A Preliminary Study with Revision of Chapter III (New York: Macmillan paperback, 1978), p. 164.

[2] C. S. Lewis, "Modern Theology and Biblical Criticism," Christan Reflections, ed. Walter Hooper (Grand Rapids: William B. Eerdmans, 1967), p. 153.

[3] Lewis, Miracles, p. 164.

[4] Albert Schweitzer, The Quest of the Historical Jesus (New York: The Macmillan Co., 1961), p. 16.

[5] Rudolf Bultmann, Jesus and the Word (New York: Charles Scribner's Sons, 1934), p. 8.

[6] Rudolf Bultmann, Primitive Christianity in its Contemporary Setting (New York: Meridian, 1956), p. 200.

[7] Rudolf Bultmann, Theology of the New Testament, trans. Kendrick Grobel (S.C.M. Press, 1952), I, p.30.

[8] Lewis, Christian Reflections, p. 156.

[9] Lewis, Christian Reflections, p. 157.

[10] Lewis, Christian Reflections, p. 157.

[11] Adolf von Harnack, What is Christianity? (New York: Harper and Row, 1957), p. 52.

[12] Harnack, p. 14.

[13] Harnack, p. 14.

[14] C. S. Lewis, Mere Christianity, (New York: Macmillan paperback, 1960), p. 55

[15] C. S. Lewis, "What are We to Make of Jesus Christ?," God in the Dock, ed. Walter Hooper (Grand Rapids: William B. Eerdmans, 1970), p. 159.

[16] Lewis, Mere Christianity, p. 56.

[17] C. S. Lewis, The Screwtape Letters: with

Screwtape Proposes a Toast (New York: Macmillan paperback, 1975), pp. 106-108.

[18]Schweitzer, The Quest of the Historical Jesus, pp. 370-71.

[19]C. S. Lewis, The World's Last Night: and Other Essays (New York: Harcourt Brace Jovanovich, 1960), pp. 95-96.

[20]Lewis, Last Night, pp. 96-97.

[21]Lewis, Last Night, p. 98.

[22]Lewis, Last Night, p. 98-99.

[23]Lewis, Last Night, p. 100.

[24]Rudolf Bultmann, "New Testament and Mythology," in Kerygma and Myth, ed. H. W. Bartsch, (New York: Harper and Row, 1961), p. 5.

[25]Lewis, Last Night, p. 101.

[26]Lewis, Last Night, p. 106.

[27]Lewis, Last Night, p. 111.

[28]Bultmann, Kerygma and Myth, p. 5.

[29]Lewis, Miracles, p. 4.

[30]Lewis, Miracles, p. 5.

[31]Lewis, Miracles, p. 68.

[32]Lewis, Miracles, p. 47.

[33]Lewis, Miracles, p. 60.

[34]Chad Walsh, The Literary Legacy of C. S. Lewis (New York: Harcourt Brace Jovanovich, 1979) p. 215.

[35]Lewis, Miracles, p. 132.

[36]Lewis, Miracles, p. 133.

[37]Lewis, Miracles, p. 145.

[38] Lewis, Miracles, p. 145.

[39] Lewis, Miracles, p. 160-161.

[40] C. S. Lewis, "Horrid Red Things," God in the Dock, p. 69.

[41] Schweitzer, The Quest of the Historical Jesus, p. 13.

[42] Hugh Anderson, ed., Jesus: Great Lives Observed, (Englewood Cliffs, N.J.: Prentice-Hall, 1967), p. 10.

[43] John Locke, The Reasonableness of Christianity, ed. I. T. Ramsey (Stanford, 1958), p. 80.

[44] Norman Perrin, What is Redaction Criticism?, (Philadelphia: Fortress Press, 1969), p. 12.

[45] Bultmann, Theology of the New Testament, p. 30.

[46] Lewis, Christian Reflections, pp. 155-156.

[47] Lewis, Christian Reflections, p. 155.

[48] Lewis, Christian Reflections, p. 158.

[49] Lewis, Christian Reflections, p. 158.

[50] Lewis, Christian Reflections, p. 159.

[51] Lewis, Christian Reflections, p. 160.

[52] Lewis, Christian Reflections, p. 160.

[53] Lewis, Christian Reflections, p. 161.

[54] C. S. Lewis, Letters to Malcolm: Chiefly on Prayer (New York: Harcourt Brace Jovanovich, 1964), p. 47.

[55] Lewis, Malcolm, p. 47.

[56] Lewis, Miracles, p. 148.

[57] Chad Walsh, C. S. Lewis: Apostle to the Skeptics (New York: The Macmillan Co., 1949), pp. 93-94.

[58] Christensen, Michael J., C. S. Lewis on

Scripture: His Thoughts on the Nature of Biblical Inspiration, the Role of Revelation and the Question of Inerrancy (Waco, Texas: Word Books, 1979), pp. 97-98.

[59] C. H. Dodd, The Interpretation of the Fourth Gospel (Cambridge: Cambridge University Press, 1953), p. 445-446.

[60] Lewis, God in the Dock, p. 159.

[61] Walter Lock, "The Gospel According to St. John," in A New Commentary on Holy Scripture, including the Apocrypha, ed. Charles Gore, Henry Leighton Goudge, Alfred Guillaume (London: S.P.C.K., 1928), p. 241.

[62] Lewis, Christian Reflections, p. 155.

[63] Humphrey Carpenter, The Inklings: C. S. Lewis, J. R. R. Tolkien, Charles Williams, and Their Friends (Boston: Houghton Mifflin, 1978), p. 216.

[64] Peter J. Schakel, Reason and Imagination in C. S. Lewis (Grand Rapids: William B. Eerdmans, 1984), p. 149.

[65] C. S. Lewis, "Christian Apologetics," God in the Dock, p. 103.

[66] Schakel, Reason and Imagination in C. S. Lewis, p. 150.

[67] Schakel, Reason and Imagination in C. S. Lewis, p. 150.

[68] Walsh, The Literary Legacy of C. S. Lewis, p. 251.

CHAPTER FOUR

CHRIST AND ASLAN

Lewis's conversion to Christianity involved a recognition of both the mythic and historical elements of the Christian faith. Although Lewis attempted to make a strong case for the <u>historical</u> nature of the Gospels, perhaps it was Lewis's view of myth which was most helpful in his defense of Christianity. That Jesus came alive for Lewis in the Gospels is evident from his comments about Him. That Lewis was able to give life to a fictional "Christ figure" is evident in his <u>Narnia Chronicles</u>. Interestingly enough, it is in his fictional writings that Lewis seemed most expressive about the nature of Christ and most expansive about what the Incarnation means. Lewis himself admitted as much: "Why did one find it so hard to feel as one was told one ought to feel about God or about the sufferings of Christ? I thought the chief reason was that one was told one ought to. An obligation to feel can freeze feelings. . . . But supposing that by casting all these things into an imaginary world, stripping them of their stained-glass and Sunday school associations, one could make them for the first time appear in their real potency? Could one not thus steal past those watchful dragons? I thought one could."[1]

Thus, Lewis created for his <u>Chronicles of Narnia</u> a fictional equivalent of Christ. Aslan is "an invention giving an imaginary answer to the question, 'What might Christ become like, if there really were a world like Narnia and He chose to be incarnate and die and rise again in <u>that</u> world rather than ours?'"[2]

In order to fully understand Lewis's view of Christianity as "myth become fact," it is helpful to examine both his view of the historical Jesus and how he recreated this historical figure into an image of the mythical beast called "Aslan." In comparing and contrasting these two visions, one may learn more about not only Lewis's views concerning Jesus but also his views concerning the mythic power of the Christian story.

In his discussion of the historical Jesus, Lewis

wrestled with the problem of how a man could maintain his humanity while at the same time becoming the Incarnation of God. In a private letter written in 1947, Lewis attempted to explain the relationship of Humanity and Divinity in the person of Jesus. Lewis first concluded that the doctrine that Jesus was God did not mean that He was a human body with a divine soul. Instead, it meant "that a real man (human body <u>and</u> human soul) was in Him so united with the second Person of the Trinity as to make one Person: just as in you and me a complete anthropoid animal (animal body <u>and</u> animal 'soul,' i.e. instincts, sensations, etc.) is so united with an immortal rational soul as to be one person."[3] In other words, declared Lewis, if the Divine Son had been removed from Jesus what would have been left would have been not a corpse but a living man.

This concept of Lewis's is congruent with the "two natures--one person" creed developed by the Council of Chalcedon in 451: "One and the same Christ, Son, Lord, Only-begotten, proclaimed in two natures, without confusion, without change, without division, without separation; the difference of the natures being in no way destroyed on account of the union, but rather the peculiar property of each nature being preserved and concurring in one person and one hypostasis." Thus, wrote Lewis elsewhere, "men can read the life of Our Lord (because it is a human life) as nothing but a human life."[4]

Lewis stressed that although the human soul in Jesus was "unswervingly united to the God in Him in that which makes a personality one, namely Will, it had the <u>feelings</u> of any normal man; hence could be tempted, could fear etc."[5] Lewis was concerned that Christians avoid the Docetist heresy, which declared that Jesus only seemed to be human. For Lewis, the Incarnation meant entering into the full experience of humanity, and by entering this experience perceiving and in the literal meaning of the word "sensing" the world from a human point of view. As Lewis characterized it, Jesus was born into the world as an actual man, "a real man of a particular height, with hair of a particular colour, speaking a particular language, weighing so many stone."[6]

For Lewis, this entering into humanity of the Divine involved in some sense a humiliation, a reduction of the Divine to the confines of a lesser level of Being. As he depicted it: "The Eternal Being. . . became not only a man but (before that) a baby, and before that a foetus inside a Woman's body. If you want to get the hang of it, think how you would like to become a slug or a crab."[7]

This process of incarnation meant that Jesus suffered from the limits of other human beings, at least in terms of perceptions and understanding, for otherwise, said Lewis, he would not be fully human. As Lewis pictured it: "It might be argued that when He emptied Himself of His glory He also humbled Himself to share, as man, the current superstitions of His time. And I certainly think that Christ, in the flesh, was not omniscient--if only because a human brain could not, presumably, be the vehicle of omniscient consciousness, and to say that Our Lord's thinking was not really conditioned by the size and shape of His brain might be to deny the real Incarnation and become a Docetist."[8]

For Lewis, Jesus's humanity meant even the possibility of mis-statements of fact or misconceptions, caused in part by the world view of his time. Lewis stated, "If Our Lord had committed Himself to any scientific or historical statement which He knew to be untrue, this would not disturb my faith in His deity."[9]

Not only was Jesus vulnerable to misconceptions, declared Lewis, He was also vulnerable to temptation. As Lewis wrote in a letter to Arthur Greeves, "When it says God can't be tempted I take this to be an obvious truth. God, as God, can't, any more than He can die. He became man precisely to do and suffer what as God He could not do and suffer."[10]

For Lewis, Jesus's triumph was not that He did not experience temptation, but that He did not succumb to it. As Lewis wrote in a private letter to Owen Barfield, "If we are to accept the Gospels. . . we must interpret Christ's perfection in a sense which admits of his feeling _both_ the commonest and most animal temptations (hunger and the fear of death) _and_ those temptations which usually occur only to the worst of men (devil-worship for the sake of power)."[11]

Even Jesus's emotional makeup was touched on by Lewis to indicate Jesus's full humanity. Lewis stressed that Jesus was not a Stoic savior but one who fully experienced the whole gamut of emotions, from joy to despair. As Lewis wrote in a private letter, "God could, had He pleased, have been incarnate in a man of iron nerves, the Stoic sort who lets no sigh escape him. Of His great humility, He chose to be incarnate in a man of delicate sensibilities who wept at the grave of Lazarus and sweated blood in Gethsemane. Otherwise we should have missed the great lesson that it is by his will alone that a man is good or bad, and that feelings are not, in themselves, of any importance."[12]

What makes Jesus unique for Lewis is not his emotional makeup but the nature of his "will." Jesus's refusal to submit to temptation and weakness, in spite of his human feelings and fears, provides the model of behavior for the believer. Lewis wrote in The Problem of Pain: "Christian renunciation does not mean stoic 'Apathy,' but a readiness to prefer God to inferior ends which are in themselves lawful. Hence the Perfect Man brought to Gethsemane a will, and a strong will, to escape suffering and death if such escape were compatible with the Father's will, combined with a perfect readiness for obedience if it were not."[13]

Again, as Lewis wrote in private correspondence, "He has faced all that the weakest of us face, has shared not only the strength of our nature but every weakness of it except sin. If He had been incarnate in a man of immense natural courage, that would have been for many of us almost the same as His not being incarnate at all."[14]

Lewis also rejected the view that Jesus saw his death as a type of "liberation." As he wrote to one correspondent, "Your idea of Christ as suffering from the mere fact of being in the body, and therefore tempted--if at all--to hasten rather than postpone his death, seems to imply that he was not (as the Christian mystery runs) 'perfect God and perfect man,' but a kind of composite being . . . an archangel imprisoned in a vehicle unsuitable to it (like Ariel in the oak) and in constant revolt against that vehicle. This is mythological in the bad sense."[15]

For Lewis, what was truly remarkable about Christ was that in Him one had a man who really was what all men were intended to be. As Lewis depicted it in Mere Christianity, "The natural human creature in Him was taken up fully into the divine Son. . . . And then, after being thus killed--killed every day in a sense--the human creature in Him, because it was united to the divine Son, came to life again. The Man in Christ rose again: not only the God. That is the whole point. For the first time we saw a real man."[16]

But what of Jesus's teachings themselves? What insight into the personality of Jesus do these teachings give us? Lewis did not over-exaggerate the literary value of their style: "The same divine humility which decreed that God should become a baby at a peasant-woman's breast and later an arrested field-preacher in the hands of the Roman police, decreed also that He should be preached in a vulgar, prosaic and unliterary language. If you can stomach the one, you can stomach the other. The Incarnation is in that sense an irreverent doctrine: Christianity in that sense an irreverent religion."[17]

For Lewis, an over-emphasis on the literary quality of the Gospel teachings takes away from the insight they give us into the nature and character of Jesus. As Lewis wrote in a discussion of Jesus's poetic style, "I dread an over-emphasis on the poetical elements in His words because I think it tends to obscure that quality in His human character which is, in fact, so visible in His irony, His argumenta ad homines, and His use of the a fortiori, and which I would call the homely, peasant shrewdness. Donne points out that we are never told He laughed; it is difficult in reading the Gospels not to believe, and to tremble in believing, that He smiled."[18]

Lewis admitted that Jesus's moral teachings as such were not particularly unique. As he portrayed it, "What is common to Zarathustra, Jeremiah, Socrates, Gautama, Christ and Marcus Aurelius, is something pretty substantial."[19] Also, Lewis declared, Jesus was never regarded solely as a moral teacher. Lewis commented, "He did not produce that effect on any of the people who actually met Him. He produced three effects--Hatred--Terror--Adoration. There was no trace of people expressing mild approval."[20]

Still, it is through Jesus's teachings that we get the clearest insight into Jesus's personality. These teachings, Lewis pointed out, are many times in the forms of Jewish poetry common to the Israel of Jesus's day. Although not wanting to over-emphasize the poetic element, Lewis stated its importance: "Our Lord, soaked in the poetic tradition of His country, delighted to use it. . . . I think, too, it will do us no harm to remember that, in becoming Man, He bowed His neck beneath the sweet yoke of a heredity and early environment. Humanly speaking, He would have learned this style, if from no one else (but it was all about Him) from his mother."[21]

After citing Mary's <u>Magnificat</u> as an example of Hebrew poetry's parallelism, Lewis concluded, "There is a fierceness, even a touch of Deborah, mixed with the sweetness in the <u>Magnificat</u> to which most painted Madonnas do little justice; matching the frequent severity of his <Jesus's> own sayings. I am sure the private life of the holy family was, in many senses, 'mild' and 'gentle', but perhaps hardly in the way some hymn writers have in mind. One may suspect, on proper occasions, a certain astringency; and all in what people at Jerusalem regarded as a rough north-country dialect."[22]

This toughness, found in many of Jesus's parables and sayings, breaks through the pious preconceptions of Jesus as the "meek and mild" savior. As Lewis analyzed it, "Our Lord's own words are both far fiercer and far more tolerable than those of the theologians. He says nothing about guarding against earthly loves for fear we might be hurt; He says something that cracks like a whip about trampling them all under foot the moment they hold us back from following Him."[23]

Of course, Jesus's strongest denunciations were reserved not for the lowest elements of society, the 'tax-collectors and sinners', but for those that were considered to be the most religious. This, Lewis saw, was the result of Jesus's perception that the most significant danger of all is the sin of pride. As Lewis stated, "The dangers of apparent self-sufficiency explain why Our Lord regards the vices of the feckless and dissipated so much more leniently than the vices that lead to worldly success. Prostitutes are in no danger of finding their present life so satisfactory that they cannot turn to God: the proud, the avaricious, the self-righteous, are in that danger."[24]

Lewis also pointed out that Jesus's teachings were not, in a philosophical sense, a system of thought at all. Lewis observed, "The teaching of Our Lord Himself. . . is not given us in that cut-and-dried, fool-proof systematic fashion we might have expected or desired. He wrote no book. We have only reported sayings, most of them uttered in answer to questions, shaped in some degree by their context."[25]

As Lewis perceived it, Jesus's teachings could only be understood by giving the response of the whole man, not merely of the intellect. The problem that Lewis had with many of the Nineteenth Century "lives" of Jesus was that they selected certain teachings of Jesus while ignoring others, thus conceiving of Him as an idealistic philosopher, a romantic, or a social revolutionary. This approach imposed upon these teachings a system of thought foreign to Jesus's method. Lewis argued: "He preaches, but He does not lecture. He uses paradox, proverb, exaggeration, parable, irony; even (I mean no irreverence) the 'wisecrack.' He utters maxims which, like popular proverbs, if rigorously taken may seem to contradict one another. His teaching therefore cannot be grasped by the intellect alone, cannot be 'got up' as if it were a 'subject.' If we try to do that with it, we shall find Him the most elusive of teachers. He hardly ever gave a straight answer to a straight question. He will not be, in the way we want, 'pinned down.' The attempt is (again I mean no irreverence) like trying to bottle a sunbeam."[26]

Although Lewis admitted that one may respect, and at moments envy, both the Fundamentalist's view of the Bible and the Roman Catholic view of the Church, neither position recognizes the elusiveness of Jesus's own teaching. In taking the Bible literally one may miss the deeper, spiritual truths, the truths that can only be expressed in poetry and myth. As Lewis majestically portrayed it, "There is almost no 'letter' in the words of Jesus. Taken by a literalist, He will always prove the most elusive of teachers. Systems cannot keep up with that darting illumination. No net less wide than a man's whole heart, nor less fine of mesh than love, will hold the sacred fish."[27]

In spite of Lewis's admissions that Jesus, as man, was limited to some degree by his human nature, culture, and surroundings, Lewis, as stated previously, affirmed Jesus's full Divinity. This was also seen by Lewis as Jesus's self-understanding, not something imposed by the early church after Jesus's resurrection. Lewis cited Jesus's own comments as evidence of this self-concept: "He told people that their sins were forgiven, and never waited to consult all the other people whom their sins had undoubtedly injured. He unhesitatingly behaved as if He was the party chiefly concerned, the person chiefly offended in all offences. This makes sense only if He really was the God whose laws are broken and whose love is wounded in every sin. In the mouth of any speaker who is not God, these words would imply what I can only regard as a silliness and conceit unrivalled by any other character in history."[28]

Yet, this same Person is seen as being 'humble and meek,' by those around him, and by those who read the Gospel accounts: "Even his enemies, when they read the Gospels, do not usually get the impression of silliness and conceit. Still less do unprejudiced readers. Christ says that He is 'humble and meek' and we believe Him; not noticing that, if He were merely a man, humility and meekness are the very last characteristics we could attribute to some of His sayings."[29]

Thus, Lewis conceived of Jesus as being both Human and Divine, both Man and God, in a complex inter-relationship that involves both the limitations of human feelings and perceptions and the divine qualities of forgiveness and judgement. He is the prophetic voice utilizing the Hebrew poetic style, and the Divine Judge who passes judgement on Jerusalem declaring, "Truly, truly, I say to you, before Abraham was, I am (John 8:58)."

Although Lewis described Jesus's personality as being as clear in the Gospel's as Plato's Socrates or Boswell's Johnson, little of that personality appears in Lewis's non-fictional works. An analysis of

Jesus's character is scattered throughout a number of Lewis's non-fiction writings, with much of his speculation concerning the nature of Jesus appearing in private correspondences. Perhaps this is because Lewis saw himself in the role of the popular apologist, presenting the case for 'mere Christianity' without getting involved in the doctrinal disputes that separated Christian denominations or in the debate over Jesus's various prescriptions for Christian life and conduct.

Lewis felt no such constraints in his fictional writings. In various works such as <u>The Space Trilogy</u> and <u>The Chronicles of Narnia</u>, Lewis gave freer reign both to his imagination and his expressiveness. This helped bring to life his portrayal of a fictional "Christ" in a way his non-fictional works did not. Dr. Fred Graham comments on the disparity between Lewis's fictional and non-fictional writings by comparing the approach of Lewis's <u>Mere Christianity</u> and <u>Miracles</u> to <u>The Silver Chair</u>: "The problem of these <non-fictional> works does not lie in their orthodoxy. Rather it has to do with the inevitable narrowing and flattening effect, the prosaic quality that results when anyone must treat great and often paradoxical themes in brief compass. For example, the argument for God's existence in <u>Mere Christianity</u> simply doesn't work. One keeps saying, 'Yes, but. . . ' even when one is a believer. Whereas in <u>The Silver Chair</u> the nearly successful effort to convince the children and Puddleglum that there is no sky, no Lion, reveals to the reader the deadly asphyxiating stuffiness of life without the transcendent. . . . The children's story pricks our imagination; it works. The proof for God's existence in <u>Mere Christianity</u> does not."[30]

To fully understand Lewis's concept of Christ it is necessary to examine that concept in Lewis's fictional settings. Lewis's most notable "Christ figures" in his imaginative fiction are the <u>Chronicles of Narnia</u>'s Aslan, and <u>Out of the Silent Planet</u>'s Maledil. Each figure is a representation of God, but each differs noticeably in role and function.

In Lewis's science fictional work describing an imaginary trip to Mars, Maledil first appears as the deity of the inhabitants of Malacandra (the native's name for our Mars). When he is first discovered by

Ransom, the hero of the novel, Maledil seems to be the deity of that planet alone, but as the other two stories of The Space Trilogy unfold he is shown to have dominion over all of the planets of the solar system, excluding only the fallen planet Thulcandra, which is Earth. As Robert Houston Smith pointed out, Maledil serves a function somewhat like that of a Stoic logos.[31]

Maledil is shown as a creating, acting, governing deity, a lawgiver and a strict, though loving, judge. He is, however, neither seen nor heard by Ransom or by most of the creatures on Malacandra and is not said to have had any creaturely incarnation on that planet. He does apparently speak to the governing spirit of Malacandra, and in Perelandra he is said to speak directly to the two humanoids that inhabit Venus, much as God is said to have talked with Adam and Eve in Eden. As R. H. Smith stated, "The figure functions somewhat as the Holy Spirit does in the Christian tradition."[32]

Lewis indicated that Maledil may have had a role in fashioning the planetary system, and that Maledil came to Earth in the person of Christ: "In the fallen World He prepared for himself a body and was united with the Dust and made it glorious for ever."[33] For the inhabitants of earth, he serves as a redeemer. The inhabitants of Malacandra and Perelandra (Venus) have no need for redemption for they had never fallen into sin.

Lewis touched on this same theme in a non-fiction article in the Christian Herald entitled "Will We Lose God in Outer Space?"[34] Lewis proposed that space travel might challenge the basic Christian tenet of man's uniqueness. There could be rational species for whom Christ's incarnation and sacrifice would be irrelevant. God would have made a different covenant with them. As Dabney Adams Hart noted: "Whatever the theologians made of Lewis's speculations, the connection with his novels and children's stories was clear. The non-human rational and spiritual creatures in his fiction, profoundly true as images, might prove closer to fact than he or his readers had imagined. However surprising the Christian Herald article may have been for some readers of Lewis's religious works, any who had understood his novels recognized a similar theme."[35]

In *Perelandra*, the young King of Venus describes his theological education by stating "I learned. . . about Maledil and about His Father and the Third One."[36] Thus, Lewis even alluded to the Christian Trinity. Still, as Smith pointed out, "In spite of Lewis's attempts to link him with Christ, Maledil remains, by virtue of his non-appearance, more of a transcendent God than a God incarnate."[37]

Part of the reason for Maledil's non-involvement is the lack of a Fall on either Malacandra or Perelandra. For the plot of the stories to develop at all, evil has to be introduced by representatives of the planet Earth. The situation is somewhat different in Lewis's children's fantasy *The Chronicles of Narnia.*

Walter Hooper stated that C. S. Lewis believed there are three elements in all developed religions, and in Christianity, one more.[38] The first is the experience of the "Numinous," the sense of awe, wonder and inadequacy one feels in the presence of the Holy. The second element in religion is the consciousness of a moral law, and the third element appears when we realize that the numinous power is the guardian of the morality to which we feel a sense of duty or obligation. The fourth element, for Lewis the uniquely Christian element, is the historical event of Christianity, the Incarnation, and the recognition that the incarnate Son of God is the "awful haunter of nature, and the giver of the moral law."[39]

All of these elements are found in Aslan, the great, golden Lion of Narnia, the God incarnate of *The Chronicles of Narnia.* As R. H. Smith indicated, in Aslan, Lewis brought together both the transcendence and immanence of God, being at once both supernatural and natural, aloof and personal, passive and active.[40]

Aslan (from the Turkish word for lion, Arslan) does not dwell in Narnia but comes to the land from a great distance when need arises. He creates, states moral values, inspires, judges, attacks evil, and rescues his followers. He can be immensely fierce, as lions tend to be, but his anger is always purposeful and just.

Aslan also has a role to play in Narnia that could not have been acted out in Lewis's science fiction worlds of Malacandra and Perelandra. Narnia is a world in which evil has existed from the day that Narnia was created. Narnia is therefore in constant need of divine assistance, whereas Malacandra and Perelandra have no need of such intervention. As R. H. Smith understood it, "It is the presence of evil that makes the fullness of the deity suddenly flame forth."[41]

Of course, the parallels between Aslan and Christ are obvious, but that is not what originally inspired Lewis to write The Narnia Chronicles. Lewis, as usual, had very little patience with those critics who tried to construct a psychological model to describe the process by which Lewis wrote his fantasy. As Lewis described them: "Some people seem to think that I began by asking myself how I could say something about Christianity to children; then fixed on the fairy tale as an instrument; then collected information about child-psychology and decided what age group I'd write for; then drew up a list of basic Christian truths and hammered out 'allegories' to embody them. This is all pure moonshine."[42]

According to Lewis, everything began with images--a faun carrying an umbrella or a queen on a sledge. At first, Lewis declared, there wasn't even anything specifically Christian about them. Lewis wrote a few pages around the start of World War II, but "at first I had very little idea of how the story would go."[43]

Lewis turned to other matters, producing the theological writings The Problem of Pain, The Screwtape Letters, and Mere Christianity. At the same time he was producing Perelandra, A Preface to Paradise Lost, That Hideous Strength, The Abolition of Man, and The Great Divorce. As Charles Huttar grasped, "To list the major themes of these works, and especially those they share in common, would be to anticipate what was preoccupying Lewis's mind during the period of writing the Chronicles of Narnia, 1949-53."[44]

Huttar saw that all through this period Lewis's mind was unconsciously preparing itself to return to these images again. By the late forties he was talking about completing a children's book which he had begun.[45] Two years later, the first five books in the series were finished. What had happened? "Suddenly Aslan came bounding into it. . . . Once He was there He pulled the whole story together, and soon He pulled the six other Narnian stories in after Him."[46]

Although Professor Tolkien once told Walter Hooper that he thought that the Christian elements in the Narnian stories were too "obvious,"[47] Lewis was not rewriting the Gospels' story in allegorical form. As Lewis replied to one reader, "I'm not exactly representing the real (Christian) story in symbols I'm more saying, 'Suppose there were a world like Narnia and it needed rescuing and the Son of God (or the Great Emperor Overseas) went to redeem it, as He came to redeem ours, what might it, in that world, all have been like?' Perhaps it comes to much the same thing as you thought but not quite."[48] As Lewis was to write in another context, "Within a given story any object, person, or place is neither more nor less nor other than what that story effectively shows it to be. The ingredients of one story cannot be anything in another story, for they are not in it at all."[49]

As Paul A. Karkainen saw it, "Because he is depicted as an animal, Aslan does not compete with Christ; he illuminates Him. The Narnia books show Christ much as the first century saw Him--with the freshness and bloom of first encounter and stripped of the banalities which have grown up around the Lord of Glory."[50]

This attempt of Lewis to get past the "watchful dragons" of religious piety and stereotyped responses was one of his purposes in writing the Chronicles. However, this attempt to restate the Christ event in mythical form may also help to illustrate Lewis's own conceptions of the nature of Jesus when Lewis was unencumbered by the role of Christian apologist.

According to Lewis critic Peter Schakel, the Chronicles' narrative technique borders on or passes completely into the realm of myth. As Schakel explicated, "the Chronicles are high myth, communicating so directly to the imagination and emotions through powerful images and symbols that they cannot be translated fully into intellectual terms."[51]

Schakel admitted that occasionally passages suggest a single allegorical meaning through references to the Bible or Christianity. But most of the time they lie "slightly to the mythic side of the dividing line," so that their primary appeal is to the imagination rather than the intellect.[52]

Schakel went on to point out that the Christianity in the <u>Chronicles</u> is deeper and more subtle than the term allegory suggests. As Schakel saw it, "When the <u>Chronicles</u> are at their best, they do not just convey Christian meanings intellectually, by 'representations', but they communicate directly to the imagination and the emotions a sizable share of the central elements of the Christian faith."[53] The use of myth allows other meanings to emanate from the stories as well, allowing the author to say "what he does not yet know and could not come by in any other way."[54]

To understand the very beginnings or "genesis" of Narnia it is necessary to read <u>The Magician's Nephew</u> (1955), actually the sixth book in the series of seven. When the children Polly Plummer and Digory Kirke accidentally arrive in Narnia, it is nothing but an expanse of cold dry darkness. At last a voice begins to sing in the distance, the most beautiful voice they had ever heard: "A voice had begun to sing. It was very far away and Digory found it hard to decide from what direction it was coming. Sometimes it seemed to come from all directions at once. Sometimes he almost thought it was coming out of the earth beneath them. Its lower notes were deep enough to be the voice of the earth herself. There were no words. There was hardly even a tune. . . . It was so beautiful he could hardly stand it."[55] As the children watch, the Voice sings a whole world into existence, part by part, and color by color. When they see the Singer, it is Aslan.

All beauties of Narnia are Aslan's creation, and all images are of his splendor. Thus, all relationships must be based on one's relation to him. Apart from him no genuine fulfillment is possible. As Gilbert Meilaender has pointed out, the secret of community in Narnia lies in the relation of each inhabitant of Narnia to Aslan.[56] Aslan deals with each individual in a unique way, but a repeated theme of <u>The Narnia Chronicles</u> is that each learns only his own story--the story of how he has been called by Aslan and what is required of him. He does not give an account of his relationship with any one person to any other person. When asked, Aslan answers "I am telling your story, not hers. I tell no-one any story but his own."[57]

Almost from the moment of its creation, evil had entered Narnia in the person of Jadis, who had been Queen of Charn (in another world) and who became the White Witch of Narnia. In Charn, rather than lose the throne, Jadis had uttered "the Deplorable Word" which resulted in Charn's destruction. As Meilaender states, "Jadis is the personification of a pride which would rather reign in hell than serve in heaven."[58]

The first of the adventures, <u>The Lion, the Witch, and the Wardrobe</u> (1950), begins about sixty years after the creation of Narnia when the Pevensie children, Peter, Edmund, Susan, and Lucy leave London because of air-raids during the war and go to stay with the now old Professor Digory Kirke in his great country mansion. One day Lucy accidentally discovers a doorway--an old but magical wardrobe--to Narnia and eventually all four of the children get in. Jadis, the White Witch is now queen of Narnia and has turned its weather to perpetual winter. The children eventually battle in the name of Aslan against the White Witch.

Among the four children there is a Judas. Edmund falls into the clutches of the evil White Witch, who has the kingdom of Narnia temporarily under her evil spell. Tempting Edmund first with enchanted Turkish Delight and later with the offer to make him a prince, Edmund betrays his brother and sisters to the White Witch. Edmund realizes his mistake, but too late, and is only saved along with the other children by the direct intervention of Aslan himself.

Later, Aslan and Edmund have a private conversation, and Edmund goes to his brother and two sisters and apologizes, receiving their forgiveness. Meanwhile, the Witch's Dwarf approaches and arranges a conference between Aslan and the Witch. The Witch summarizes the Deep Magic written on the Stone Table, an image recalling the Old Testament tablets of stone, which contains the natural law established by the

"Emperor Across the Sea" at the beginning of time. It was created at the same time as the Narnian universe and is a magic which makes moral and social order in the universe possible. Aslan himself considers the Deep Magic inviolate: "'Work against the Emperor's magic?' said Aslan turning to her <Susan> with something like a frown on his face. And nobody ever made that suggestion to him again."[59]

The White Witch declares that all traitors belong to her and that the penalty for betrayal is death. She renounces her claim on Edmund's blood only when Aslan offers himself as a substitute. As Chad Walsh pointed out, the death of Aslan at the hands of the White Witch achieves its power partly by a process of selection.[60] Many of the events of the Biblical story are repeated here. Jesus had a loyal following of women, so Aslan, on the night before his execution is accompanied by Lucy and Susan, who try to comfort him. The tone of the scene is like that on the Mount of Olives: "How slowly he walked! And his great, royal head drooped so that his nose nearly touched the grass. Presently he stumbled and gave a low moan."[61]

Aslan's atonement for Edmund's sin takes place at the Stone Table that same night. He surrenders himself to a howling mob of evil spirits and monsters, who bind him tightly, shear away his lion's mane, and then jeer and mock him as they place a muzzle on his face. Throughout this torment, Aslan never moves. Finally, before the Witch kills Aslan, she speaks her final words of triumph: "Now I will kill you instead of him as our pact was and so the Deep Magic will be appeased. But when you are dead what will prevent me from killing him as well? . . . . You have lost your own life and you have not saved his. In that knowledge, despair and die."[62]

At dawn the next morning, the children discover that Aslan is gone and the Stone Table is cracked in two. Turning they see Aslan, resurrected to life and larger than they remember him, his mane restored, and his glory returned. Aslan explains that the Witch's magic goes back only to the dawn of time. If it had extended farther back, she would have known of a Deeper Magic. When an innocent victim took a traitor's place on the Stone Table, the table itself would crack, and Death would begin working backwards. He then commands the girls to climb on his back, he restores other enemies of the Witch to life, and in a final pitched battle Aslan slays the White Witch and appoints the children Kings and Queens of Narnia.

As Peter Schakel discerned, this is the most nearly allegorical episode in the <u>Chronicles</u>. The willing sacrifice, the Biblical tone and imagery, and Aslan's subsequent return to life clearly associate him with Christ.[63] But, as Walter Hooper made clear, there are differences as well as similarities.[64] Whereas Christ is portrayed as dying on the cross for the whole world, Aslan dies for one child, Edmund. And whereas Christ is portrayed as passing after death into a life that has its own new Nature, Aslan has no such dramatic physical change after his resurrection.

As Schakel indicated, the general meaning of Aslan's death is very similar to the meaning of the death of Christ in our world, but one does not need to know or refer to the story of Christ to gain that meaning. The story itself, by moving from Deep Magic to Deeper Magic, conveys the magic of grace in a way that abstract theology cannot. Schakel concluded, "Aslan does not 'stand for' Christ; in his suppositional world he <u>is</u> Christ. His death in Narnia is similar to his death in our world because both are examples of the same archetype of the dying and returning god. And the myth in which the story is recounted conveys the basic meaning of that archetype, the divine truth of love, sacrifice, and hope."[65]

In <u>The Lion, the Witch and the Wardrobe</u> the children's initial encounter with Aslan is one of awe. A sense of mystery and excitement is created by the mere mention of his name. When the Beaver (there are talking animals in Narnia) declares "They say Aslan is on the move--perhaps has already landed," the four children experience a strong reaction: "None of the children knew who Aslan was any more than you do; but the moment the Beaver had spoken these words everyone felt quite different. . . . At the name of Aslan, each one of the children felt something jump in his inside."[66]

Lewis made it clear that Aslan is not a tame lion, and the Beavers think it ridiculous that Susan and Lucy Pevensie expect him to be safe: "Who said anything about safe? 'Course he isn't safe. But he's good. He's the King, I tell you."[67] When the children first meet Aslan, they are overcome by the sight of "the golden mane and the great, royal, solemn, overwhelming eyes."[68] Lucy realizes that Aslan has "Terrible paws. . . if he didn't know how to velvet them!"[69]

Lewis is consistent in his view of Aslan throughout the <u>Narnia Chronicles</u>. Aslan possesses the same twofold nature that Lewis attributed to Christ. The true beasthood of Aslan is made clear in <u>The Horse and His Boy</u> (1954). The horse, Bree, is stating his sophisticated, non-mythical view of Aslan's form to his friends. As Bree gets more and more involved in his philosophical discussion, his friends watch in alarm as an enormous lion approaches him from behind. Bree is explaining that when people spoke of Aslan as a lion they meant only that he was as strong as a lion or as fierce as a lion. It would be absurd to suppose, says Bree, that Aslan was a real lion. It would be disrespectful, declares Bree, because if he was a lion he would have to be a beast just like everyone else. At this point, and much to Bree's surprise, Aslan reveals himself and urges the frightened horse to test his bodily form: "You poor, proud, frightened Horse, draw near. Nearer still, my son. Do not dare not to dare. Touch me. Smell me. Here are my paws, here is my tail, these are my whiskers. I am a true beast."[70]

Aslan exhibits a stern as well as a loving and compassionate nature. This is portrayed in his first meeting with Jill in <u>The Silver Chair</u> (1953). Aslan is displeased with her for her behavior to her companion Eustace. Now Jill is alone and thirsty. She finds a stream, but a foreboding, strange lion stands between her and the water. In a voice like a man's only "deeper, wilder, and stronger; a sort of heavy, golden voice,"[71] the lion bids her to drink. Awkwardly, she asks him to go away while she drinks, but his only answer is a look and a very low growl. When Jill asks Aslan if he will promise not to do anything, he replies he will make no promises. When she then asks the question "Do you eat girls?" Aslan's reply is not reassuring: "I have swallowed up girls and boys, women and men, kings and emperors, cities and realms."[72] Then when Jill declares she will look for another stream, Aslan replies simply: "There is no other stream."[73]

Eventually Jill realizes that Aslan's sternness is the only thing that could have helped her past her pride and ignorance to some greater good which he had planned for her. As Walter Hooper explained, "It is the proof, not the weakness of his love."[74]

Like Lewis's concept of Christ, Aslan is not a "Stoic Lion", but a lion of freely expressed emotions, joys as well as sorrows, playfulness as well as judgement. Aslan's compassionate nature is seen in the book <u>The Magician's Nephew</u>. The young English boy Digory, attempting to draw attention to the fact that his mother lies dying, blurts out, "But please, please--won't you--can't you give me something that will cure Mother?"[75] Up to this point Digory had been looking at the Lion's feet. Now he looks at his face and is shocked by what he sees: tears in the Lion's eyes. Aslan responds, "My son, my son. . . I know. Grief is great. Only you and I in this land know that yet. Let us be good to one another."[76]

There are others whom Aslan is unable to help. For example, the Dwarfs in <u>The Last Battle</u> (1956) are so determined not to be taken in that they stop their ears and close their eyes against anything that can truly help them. Even when a sumptuous feast is spread before them, they see and taste only the kind of food they would expect to find in a stable. The Dwarfs are for the Dwarfs, they stubbornly repeat. As a result, Aslan gives them up to themselves at last, explaining they had chosen cunning instead of belief. "Their prison is only in their own minds, yet they are in that prison; and so afraid of being taken in that they cannot be taken out. But come, children. I have other work to do."[77]

Similarly, in <u>The Magician's Nephew</u> the self-imposed ignorance of Uncle Andrew prevents him from hearing anything except growlings and roarings when Aslan speaks: "The longer and more beautifully the Lion sang, the harder Uncle Andrew tried to make himself believe that he could hear nothing but roaring. . . . He soon did hear nothing but roaring in Aslan's song. Soon he couldn't have heard anything else even if he had wanted to."[78] Aslan is unable to teach him or comfort him, and declares: "Oh Adam's sons, how cleverly you defend yourselves against all that might do you good!"[79] Although Aslan is both awesome and beautiful, one must consciously choose to follow him.

But who must one follow once one leaves Narnia? In *The Voyage of the Dawn Treader*, when Edmund and Lucy are told they must return home, they ask Aslan if he is present there too: "I am. . . but there I have another name. You must learn to know me by that name. This was the very reason why you were brought to Narnia, that by knowing me here for a little, you may know me better there."[80]

The parallels between Christ and Aslan are apparent, but in a private letter to a young girl, Lewis pointed out that there are differences as well as similarities: "The creation of Narnia is the Son of God creating <u>a</u> world (not specially <u>our</u> world) . . . . The stone table <u>is</u> meant to remind one of Moses' table. . . . The Passion and Resurrection of Aslan are the Passion and Resurrection Christ might be supposed to have had in <u>that</u> world--like those in our world but not exactly like. . . . At the very edge of the Narnian world Aslan begins to appear more like Christ as He is known in <u>this</u> world. Hence, the Lamb. Hence, the breakfast--like at the end of St. John's Gospel. Does not He say 'You have been allowed to know me in <u>this</u> world so that you may know me better when you get back to your own'? . . . . And of course the Ape and Puzzle, just before the Last Judgement (in *The Last Battle*) are like the coming of the Antichrist before the end of our world."[81]

In choosing a lion as a Christ-figure in a children's fantasy, Lewis gave himself a freedom for character development that he seemed reluctant to apply to the historical Jesus. Of course the use of a lion as a symbol of power is found in both the Old and New Testament. Hosea likens the roaring of a lion to the wrath of God: "They shall go after the Lord,/ he will roar like a lion; yea he will roar,/ and his sons shall come trembling from the West (Hosea 12:10)." In the New Testament's Revelation the lion is used as a specific symbol of Christ: "Then one of the elders said to me, 'Weep not; lo, the Lion of the tribe of Judah, the Root of David, has conquered, so that he can open the scroll and its seven seals (Revelation 5:5)."

However, as Chad Walsh indicated, the lion is the noblest of the beasts, but at the same time a lion looks "remarkably like a magnified kitten."[82] Aslan can roar with the authority of the universe but at other times he can take children riding on his back or play with them in a mock cat fight. Walsh continued: "He is ultimate power, ultimate gentleness, ultimate goodness, even ultimate cuddlesomeness. Without Aslan, we would have simply stories of cute talking animals with a few human beings scattered in. . . . The presence of Aslan introduces and sustains the additional dimension that makes the Chronicles of Narnia more than a series of adventures and marvels; Lewis infuses them with the spirit of great myth."[83]

As Charles Huttar explicated, the parallels between Christ and Aslan are many.[84] Each is the Son of the Highest and his emissary to the world, each knows sorrow, each is killed as an innocent substitute for the guilty and then returns to life. But Aslan dies for Edmund alone, not for the whole world. From Lewis's point of view, the Atonement of mankind is a doctrine unique to earth.

But the principle of voluntary self-sacrifice on another's behalf takes the form in Narnian as well as in earthly myth of a descent into the underworld, a journey to danger and death, to perform a rescue. This descent motif is also found in such Western literary classics as Homer's Odyssey, Virgil's Aeneid, and Dante's Inferno. Aslan submits silently to the Witch's knife, going, for all he knows, on a journey from which he will not return. He is only one example among many in The Narnia Chronicles of one who undergoes such a descent. Caspian sails to the world's end to break the spell on the three sleeping lords; Jill and Eustace and Puddleglum journey underground to rescue Prince Rilian; Lucy ventures into the Magician's room to free the Monopods from invisibility. As Huttar concluded, "All these are Christ figures; but none mean the same thing to Narnia that Christ means to human history, because Narnia is not Earth."[85]

Although these heroes of the Narnia Chronicles undergo dramatic changes in attitude and commitment Lewis does not provide a sentimental vision of repentance. In The Voyage of the Dawn Treader (1952) as a punishment for his irresponsibility, selfishness, and childishness, Eustace is turned into a dragon.

Trapped in this ugly form, he learns to value his friends and help others. Finally, one night Aslan appears to him and takes him to a mountain garden with a well in the center. There are marble steps going down into it, but before Eustace can enter the water he is told to undress. This obviously means shedding his dragon skin. Eustace begins to scratch at the scales and soon the skin begins to peel. In a minute he steps out of the skin and gets ready to go into the water. Then he notices that he is covered with another skin like the first one. Three times he peels off his dragon skin, only to find another one underneath. The lion then tells Eustace that he must let the lion undress him. Eustace is afraid of the claws but submits: "The very first tear he made was so deep that I thought it had gone right into my heart. And when he began pulling the skin off, it hurt worse than anything I've ever felt. The only thing that made me able to bear it was just the pleasure of feeling the stuff peel off."[86]

The lion then picks Eustace up and throws him into the water. Splashing around in it, Eustace finds that he is no longer a dragon, but is once again a boy. The lion then dresses him in new clothes and sends him back to the others.

The failure to repent is often shown to be the result of pride, and such pride brings divisions into Narnia. In <u>The Last Battle</u>, Shift, the wicked Ape, tries to claim that there is no real difference between Tash (the idol of the Calormenes) and Aslan. Tash, he says, is simply another name for Aslan.[87] However, as Shift learns, the conflict between loyalties is real and decisive.

In the scene of eschatological judgement at the conclusion of <u>The Last Battle</u>, a division is made between those who look on Aslan with love and those who do not. As the creatures of Narnia come up to the door of the stable at which Aslan stands, some look and find with delight the face for which they have always been searching, but others look and see only a source of fear and terror. Those that see terror veer off to the left into the nothingness created by Aslan's shadow. At that moment, they cease to be Talking Beasts. As Meilaender puts it: "In turning from Aslan they turn from their true selves; for loyalty to self in opposition to Aslan has turned out to be a self-destructive loyalty."[88]

Interestingly enough, one of those accepted in the last judgement of Aslan is Emeth a Calormene and devotee of Tash. When Emeth confessed that he was no son of Aslan's but the servant of Tash, Aslan declares: "Child, all the service thou hast done to Tash, I account as service done to me. . . . Therefore if any man swear by Tash and keep his oath for the oath's sake, it is by me that he has truly sworn, though he know it not, and it is I who reward him. And if any man do a cruelty in my name, then, though he says the name Aslan, it is Tash whom he serves and by Tash his deed is accepted."[89]

Peter Schakel commented that it is one of the greatnesses of the <u>Chronicles</u>, that although they have deeply Christian themes, they are not dependent upon Christianity.[90] A non-Christian reader can approach the stories as fairy tales, be moved by the adventures and the archetypal meanings, and not find the Christian elements obtrusive or distracting. Walsh agreed, pointing out that the earliest converts to Christianity already knew that a self-sacrificing God is needed to resolve the contradictions of existence. As Walsh put it, "When Lewis evokes Christian parallels, he is at the same time profiting by racial memories older than Christianity."[91] This is a point Lewis himself acknowledged when he stated that pagan myths of a dying and rising god were "good dreams" which foreshadowed the central event of Christianity.

Lewis believed that there had been a time when man could only approach the divine mystery through the use of the mythical imagination, with imagination being seen as a path to God and to true worship. As Lewis stated in one of his last works, <u>Letters to Malcolm: Chiefly on Prayer</u>: "When the <u>purport</u> of the <Biblical> images--what they say to our fear and hope and will and affections--seems to conflict with the theological abstractions, trust the purport of the images every time. For our abstract thinking is itself a tissue of analogies: a continual modelling of spiritual reality in legal or chemical or mechanical terms. Are these likely to be more adequate than the sensuous, organic, and personal images of Scripture? . . . The footprints of the Divine are more visible in that rich soil than across rocks or slag-heaps."[92]

Interestingly enough, Charles Huttar declared that since the <u>Chronicles of Narnia</u> are not epic, or novel, or any of the commonly known literary genres, he must offer a new label, "scripture," defining scripture as having the essential qualities of varied material loosely unified, a blend of mythography and realism, and a structure of the "grand design" of creation and fall, redemption and eschatology.[93] Walsh agreed, setting up a cosmic five-act drama paralleled in the Bible and the Chronicles:

Bible	Narnia
I. Creation of universe	Creation of Narnia
II. Struggle of Good and Evil	Aslan vs. the Witch
III. Death and resurrection of Christ	Death and resurrection of Aslan
IV. The present world, with its confused struggle of good and evil, though good has already triumphed in principle	Aslan intermittently reappears
V. The "end of the world" and the emergence of a new world	The end of the old Narnia and the coming of the new Narnia[94]

Huttar pointed out that the underlying structure of the genre "scripture" is a concept of history as linear and directional. Thus, Lewis was able to do things in <u>The Last Battle</u> that he was not able to do earlier, because it is the eschatological close of the work. As Huttar characterized it, "In thinking about Creation, Fall, and Redemption in Narnia, we had to pay attention to the many ways they differ from Earth's story as the Scriptures give it. What strikes us about the last things, and especially about Lewis's vision of heaven, is how little it differs. . . . The various worlds, real and imaginary, may be quite different at the beginning, but the end is one."[95]

Elaine Tixier commented that <u>The Chronicles of Narnia</u> rejuvenate our understanding of religion, bringing us nearer to the mystery of God and to a spiritual reality we might otherwise have been tempted to reject as outdated and uninteresting. She concluded that for Lewis "there exists a spiritual reality more real than what we call real, although we may need to use fairyland to convey an idea of what it is."[96]

Lewis likened our situation to being shut out of a reality richer and more fulfilling than we could ever imagine: "At present we are on the outside of the world, the wrong side of the door. . . . But all the leaves of the New Testament are rustling with the rumour that it will not always be so. Some day, God willing, we shall get in."[97]

The leaves of the Chronicles of Narnia also rustle with that same rumor, but they do so in a way that avoids a concern with the historical accuracy of the account. As Tixier saw it, "Whether they are 'false as history' is not an important question in a fairy tale; what is more important is whether the faith and the art that conceived them succeed in touching us and in helping us to imagine and desire what we know so little of, to recognize in the small joys of our lives the promise of a greater Joy to come. If it is so, the images become 'truth as prophecy' and Holiness lies at their core, for they are a help to our faith and they bring good news to those who wish to know."[98]

According to Dabney Adams Hart, Lewis's last book to be finished before his death, The Discarded Image (1964) epitomizes Lewis's central message about the powers and limits of the imagination.[99] The medieval model of the universe is now a "discarded image" because it no longer satisfies the conditions of our experience. We cannot understand the medieval author's intentions unless we can visualize the model from which he worked. However, Lewis's fundamental intention in reconstructing this model was to "induce us to regard all Models in the right way, respecting each and idolizing none. . . . No Model is a catalogue of ultimate realities, and none is a mere fantasy."[100] The models of the past have been "discarded" as no longer valid, but we can still respect and enjoy past models, recognizing that our own models will be outmoded some day as well. As Lewis described it, at any time in history "the great masters do not take any Model quite so seriously as the rest of us. They know that it is, after all, only a model, possibly replaceable."[101]

As Hart indicated, Lewis's idea of replacing models usually implied adding rather than discarding: since "none is a mere fantasy," all may have some value.[102] Lewis's concept of models was closely related to his ideas about myth. As Lewis depicted it in a private letter, "My view wd. be that a good myth (i.e. a story out of which ever varying meanings will grow for different readers and in different ages) is a higher thing than an allegory (into which <u>one</u> meaning has been put). Into an allegory a man can put only what he already knows; in a myth he puts what he does not yet know and cd. not come by in any other way."[103]

This realization that our models are not infallible, that our myths are parts of a greater story is found again and again in the <u>Chronicles of Narnia</u>. When the children meet Aslan after the railway accident in <u>The Last Battle</u>, he announces gently: "The term is over: the holidays have begun. The dream is ended: this is the morning."[104] Lewis then concluded this last book in the series: "the things that began to happen after that were so great and beautiful that I cannot write them. . . . For them it was only the beginning of the real story. . . the Great Story, which no one on earth has read: which goes on for ever: in which every chapter is better than the one before."[105]

Lewis, of course, was aware that the theology of the historic Christian faith may also be eventually seen as not so much wrong as inadequate: "One often wonders how different the context of our faith will look when we see it in the total context. Might it be as if one were living in an infinite earth? Further knowledge wd. leave our map of the Atlantic say, quite <u>correct</u>, but if it turned out to be the estuary of a great river--and the continent through which that river flowed turned out to be itself an island--off the shores of a still greater continent-- and so on. You see what I mean? Not one jot of Revelation will be proved false; but so many new truths might be added."[106]

Paul Tillich wrote in his book <u>Dynamics of Faith</u>

that mythological elements "should be maintained in their symbolic form and not be replaced by scientific substitutes. For there is no substitute for the use of symbols and myths: they are the language of faith."[107]

Lewis also recognized that religious myths should be examined and analyzed but not abandoned if man is to speak of ultimate reality. In An Experiment in Criticism, Lewis admitted that he has not discovered a rule by which good literature can be measured: "The nearest I have yet got to an answer is that we seek an enlargement of our being. We want to be more than ourselves."[108]

Perhaps this observation applies to religious faith as well as literature. Lewis maintained to the end of his life that Christianity was "myth become fact." But as he wrote in 1944, "Even assuming (which I most constantly deny) that the doctrines of historic Christianity are merely mythical, it is the myth which is the vital and nourishing element in the whole concern."[109]

Lewis was highly critical of any attempts to "demythologize" the New Testament. As he had written in Letters to Malcolm, "What they now call 'demythologizing' Christianity can easily be 're-mythologizing' it--and substituting a poorer mythology for a richer."[110] Lewis's writings on Christianity and his fictional works have both shown the powerful nature of Myth as a method of conveying universal truth in a way that the human imagination can comprehend. Whether Christianity is or is not "myth become fact," Lewis has shown to the reader Christianity's power as myth and has recreated that power to a lesser degree in his Narnia Chronicles.

According to Lewis, "The value of myth is that it takes all the things we know and restores to them the rich significance which has been hidden by 'the veil of familiarity.'"[111] Lewis has awakened for many a new appreciation of Christianity because he has made the familiar new again. It is in this recreation of the Christian story rather than in his logical defense of Christian dogma that Lewis is most successful.

NOTES: CHAPTER FOUR

[1] C. S. Lewis, "Sometimes Fairy Stories May Say Best What's To Be Said," in his *Of Other World: Essays and Stories*, ed. Walter Hooper (New York: Harcourt Brace Jovanovich, 1966) p. 37.

[2] "To a Lady," December 20, 1958, *Letters of C. S. Lewis*, ed. W. H. Lewis (New York: Harcourt Brace Jovanovich 1966), p. 283.

[3] "To Mrs. Frank L. Jones," Undated, 1947, *Letters of C. S. Lewis*, p. 210.

[4] C. S. Lewis, *Reflections on the Psalms* (Harcourt, Brace and World, 1958), p. 116.

[5] Lewis, *Letters*, p. 210.

[6] C. S. Lewis, *Mere Christianity* (New York: Macmillan paperback, 1960), p. 155.

[7] Lewis, *Mere Christianity*, p. 155.

[8] C. S. Lewis, *The Problem of Pain* (New York: The Macmillan Co., 1961), p. 134.

[9] Lewis, *Problem of Pain*, p. 134.

[10] C. S. Lewis, *They Stand Together: The Letters of C. S. Lewis to Arthur Greeves (1914-1963)*, ed. Walter Hooper (New York: The Macmillan Co., 1979), p. 503.

[11] "To Owen Barfield," Undated, *Letters of C. S. Lewis*, p. 189.

[12] "To Mrs. Frank L. Jones," *Letters*, p. 210.

[13] Lewis, *The Problem of Pain*, p. 113.

[14] "To Mrs. Frank L. Jones," *Letters*, p. 211.

[15] "To Owen Barfield," Undated, *Letters*, p. 191.

[16] Lewis, *Mere Christianity*, p. 155.

[17] C. S. Lewis, "Modern Translations of the Bible,"

in his *God in the Dock*, ed. Walter Hooper (Grand Rapids: William B. Eerdmans, 1970), p. 230.

[18] C. S. Lewis, "Christianity and Literature," in his *Christian Reflections*, ed. Walter Hooper (Grand Rapids: William B. Eerdmans, 1967), p. 4.

[19] Lewis, *The Problem of Pain*, p. 63.

[20] Lewis, "What are We to Make of Jesus Christ?," *God in the Dock*, p. 158.

[21] Lewis, *Reflections on the Psalms*, pp. 5-6.

[22] Lewis, *Psalms*, p. 6.

[23] C. S. Lewis, *The Four Loves* (New York: Harcourt Brace and World, 1960), p. 171.

[24] Lewis, *The Problem of Pain*, pp. 112-113.

[25] Lewis, *Reflections on the Psalms*, pp. 112-113.

[26] Lewis, *Psalms*, p. 113.

[27] Lewis, *Psalms*, p. 119.

[28] Lewis, *Mere Christianity*, p. 55.

[29] Lewis, *Mere Christianity*, p. 55.

[30] W. Fred Graham, "Fantasy in a World of Monochrome: Where C.S. Lewis Continues to Help," *The Christian Century*, 92 (November 26, 1975), p.1081.

[31] Robert Houston Smith, *Patches of Godlight: The Pattern of Thought of C.S. Lewis* (Athens: University of Georgia Press, 1981), p. 70.

[32] Smith, p. 70.

[33] C. S. Lewis, *Perelandra* (New York: Macmillan paperback, 1960), p.215.

[34] C. S. Lewis, "Will We Lose God in Outer Space," *The Christian Herald*, 81 (April 1958), pp. 74-75.

[35] Dabney Adams Hart, *Through the Open Door: A New Look at C. S. Lewis* (University Alabama: University of

Alabama Press, 1984), p. 9.

[36] Lewis, *Perelandra*, p. 210.

[37] Smith, *Patches of Godlight*, p. 70.

[38] Walter Hooper, *Past Watchful Dragons: The Narnian Chronicles of C.S. Lewis* (New York: Collier Books, 1979), p. 94.

[39] Lewis, *The Problem of Pain*, p. 23.

[40] Smith, *Patches of Godlight*, p. 71.

[41] Smith, p. 73.

[42] Lewis, *Of Other Worlds*, p. 36.

[43] Lewis, *Of Other Worlds*, p. 42.

[44] Charles A. Huttar, "C. S. Lewis's Narnia and the 'Grand Design'," *The Longing for a Form: Essays on the Fiction of C. S. Lewis*, ed. Peter J. Schakel (Grand Rapids: Baker Book House, 1979), p. 122.

[45] Chad Walsh, *C. S. Lewis: Apostle to the Skeptics* (New York: The Macmillan Co., 1949), p. 10.

[46] Lewis, *Of Other Worlds*, p. 42.

[47] Walter Hooper, "Narnia: The Author, the Critics, and the Tale," *The Longing for a Form*, p. 110.

[48] Hooper, *Past Watchful Dragons*, p. 109.

[49] C. S. Lewis, "The Genesis of a Medieval Book," in his *Studies in Medieval and Renaissance Literature*, ed. Walter Hooper (London: Cambridge University Press, 1966), pp. 39-40.

[50] Paul A. Karkainen, *Narnia Explored* (Old Tappan N.J.: Fleming H. Revell Co., 1979), p. 18.

[51] Peter J. Schakel, *Reading with the Heart: The Way into Narnia* (Grand Rapids: William B. Eerdmans, 1979), p. 5

[52] Schakel, *Reading with the Heart*, p. 5.

⁵³Schakel, Heart, p. 5.

⁵⁴"To Fr. Peter Milward," September 22, 1956, Letters of C. S. Lewis, p. 271.

⁵⁵Lewis, Magician's Nephew, pp. 98-99.

⁵⁶Gilbert Meilaender, The Taste for the Other: The Social and Ethical Thought of C.S. Lewis (Grand Rapids: Willaim B. Eerdmans, 1978), p. 45.

⁵⁷Lewis, The Horse and His Boy, p. 159.

⁵⁸Meilaender, The Taste for the Other, p. 46.

⁵⁹Lewis, Wardrobe, p. 140.

⁶⁰Chad Walsh, The Literary Legacy of C. S. Lewis, (New York: Harcourt Brace Jovanovich 1979) p. 143.

⁶¹Lewis, Wardrobe, p. 147.

⁶²Lewis, Wardrobe, p. 152.

⁶³Schakel, Reading with the Heart, p. 27.

⁶⁴Hooper, Past Watchful Dragons, pp. 63-64.

⁶⁵Schakel, Reading with the Heart, pp. 27-28.

⁶⁶C. S. Lewis, The Lion, the Witch, and the Wardrobe, (New York: Collier Books, 1970) p. 64.

⁶⁷Lewis, Wardrobe, pp. 75-76.

⁶⁸Lewis, Wardrobe, p. 123.

⁶⁹Lewis, Wardrobe, p. 125.

⁷⁰C. S. Lewis, The Horse and His Boy (New York: Collier Books, 1970), p. 193.

⁷¹C. S. Lewis, The Silver Chair (New York: Collier Books, 1970), p. 16.

⁷²Lewis, Silver Chair, p. 17.

⁷³Lewis, Silver Chair, p. 17.

[74] Hooper, Past Watchful Dragons, p. 97.

[75] C. S. Lewis, The Magician's Nephew (New York: Collier Books, 1970), p. 142.

[76] Lewis, Magician's Nephew, p. 142.

[77] C. S. Lewis, The Last Battle (New York: Collier Books, 1970), p. 148.

[78] Lewis, The Magician's Nephew, p. 126.

[79] Lewis, Magician's Nephew, p. 171.

[80] Lewis, The Voyage of the "Dawn Treader", p. 216.

[81] Hooper, Past Watchful Dragons, pp. 109-110.

[82] Walsh, The Literary Legacy of C.S. Lewis, p. 137.

[83] Walsh, Legacy, p. 137.

[84] Huttar, Longing for a Form, p. 131.

[85] Huttar, p. 131.

[86] C. S. Lewis, The Voyage of the "Dawn Treader" (New York: Collier Books, 1970), p. 90.

[87] Lewis, The Last Battle, p. 31.

[88] Meilaender, The Taste for the Other, p. 47.

[89] Lewis, The Last Battle, pp. 64-65.

[90] Schakel, Reading with the Heart, p. 132.

[91] Walsh, The Literary Legacy of C.S. Lewis, p. 91.

[92] C. S. Lewis, Letters to Malcolm: Chiefly on Prayer (New York: Harcourt Brace Jovanovich, 1964) p. 52.

[93] Huttar, Longing for a Form, p. 121.

[94] Walsh, The Literary Legacy of C.S. Lewis, p. 146.

[95] Huttar, Longing for a Form, p. 121.

[96] Elaine Tixier, "Imagination Baptized, or, 'Holiness' in the Chronicles of Narnia," Longing for a Form, p. 150.

[97] C. S. Lewis, The Weight of Glory and Other Addresses; Revised and Expanded Edition, ed. Walter Hooper (New York: Macmillan paperback, 1980) p. 13.

[98] Tixier, Longing for a Form, p. 154.

[99] Hart, Through the Open Door, p. 128.

[100] C. S. Lewis, The Discarded Image: An Introduction to Medieval and Renaissance Literature, (London: Cambridge University Press, 1964) p. 222.

[101] Lewis, Discarded Image, p. 14.

[102] Hart, Through the Open Door, p. 130.

[103] "To Fr. Peter Milward," September 22, 1956, Letters of C. S. Lewis, p. 271.

[104] Lewis, The Last Battle, p. 183.

[105] Lewis, Last Battle, pp. 183-184.

[106] "To Dom Bede Griffiths, O.S.B.," February 8, 1956, Letters of C. S. Lewis, p. 267.

[107] Paul Tillich, Dynamics of Faith (New York: Harper and Row, Torchbook ed., 1958), p. 51.

[108] C. S. Lewis, An Experiment in Criticism (London: Cambridge University Press, 1961), p. 137.

[109] Lewis, "Myth Become Fact," God in the Dock, p. 64.

[110] Lewis, Letters to Malcolm, p. 52.

[111] C. S. Lewis, "The Dethronement of Power," Time and Tide, 36 (Oct. 22,1955), p. 1374.

CHAPTER FIVE

THE TRUTH OF MYTH

Lewis's conversion to Christianity involved a recognition of both the mythic and historical elements of the Christian faith. This recognition was to guide him throughout his life in his writings on Christianity. When asked in 1963 whether his views of Christ's nature had changed in the last twenty years Lewis replied, "I would say there is no substantial change."[1] Lewis did not accept the developments of Biblical scholarship made during his lifetime and largely ignored the major theological movements of the Twentieth Century. Instead, he steeped himself in the classical Christian writers of the past and showed a marked suspicion for what he called the modern trend to "chronological snobbery." This tendency of Lewis to ignore current theological movements gave him both the strength of an originality of approach that seemed to rise above the controversies of his day and the weakness of an inadequate understanding of much of the results of Biblical research.

In spite of Lewis's suspicions of modern Biblical scholarship, he failed to prove his own case that the New Testament record is completely valid <u>historically</u>. But Lewis never claimed to be either a New Testament scholar or a historian. In fact, Lewis exhibited a remarkable skepticism concerning the historical method's ability to recreate the historical. As he depicted it, "At every tick of the clock, in every inhabited part of the world, an unimaginable richness and variety of 'history' falls off the world into total oblivion. . . . When once we have realized what 'the past as it really was' means, we must freely admit that most--that nearly all--history. . . is and will remain, wholly unknown to us."[2]

Lewis's skepticism about the historical method would be unremarkable except for his claim that Christianity must be demonstrated to be true <u>historically</u>, as myth become fact. Perhaps Lewis put too much emphasis on the historicity of the Gospel record and not enough on its mythic nature. After all, Lewis had written: "Even assuming (which I most constantly deny) that the doctrines of historic Christianity are merely mythical, it is the myth which is the vital and nourishing element in the whole concern."[3]

The ambiguous nature of the results of the historical research into the Gospels has led other Christians to attempt to preserve the values of the Christian tradition while being open to the results of Biblical research. One of the most creative approaches to the redefinition of Christianity was made by Rudolf Bultmann. Bultmann attempted to interpret Christianity in such a way that one could be radically skeptical about the factual content of the Gospel narrative while continuing to believe in the essential message of the New Testament. Although Bultmann rejected attempts to reaffirm what he considered to be the outworn mythology and cosmology of the First Century Christian Church, he also believed that hidden in the mythical language of the New Testament lay a supreme truth. Bultmann declared: "Let us abandon the mythological conceptions precisely because we want to retain their deeper meaning."[4]

Bultmann believed that the message of Christianity could be disengaged from its mythical setting, not by penetrating behind the myth to some historical truth, but by taking the myth as it stands and attempting to restate it in a form free from mythical ideas. This task of reconstruction Bultmann called "demythologizing." Bultmann described demythologizing as follows: "Its aim is not to eliminate the mythological statements but to interpret them. It is a method of hemeneutics."[5]

Bultmann saw himself in the role of translator. The message of the New Testament must be translated out of the mythical language in which it has been handed down into a language which is intelligible to the modern age.

For Bultmann, to demythologize was to translate mythical language into existential language. Bultmann found the philosophy of Martin Heidegger as useful for this purpose. Bultmann saw in the categories which Heidegger developed in his existentialist work <u>Sein und Zeit</u> <Being and Time> the tools which Bultmann could use in his approach to the New Testament. Heidegger's contrast between authentic and inauthentic existence could be seen as corresponding to the New Testament's contrast between salvation and "the world," and his sense of man's fallenness could be seen as corresponding to Paul's concept of "the flesh," and "sin."

Similarly, to believe in "the cross" was to give up self-sufficiency and to live by the grace of the unseen, to be at one with one's true self and God. This is also experienced as resurrection, the beginning of new life. The cross confronts a person with a decision. He must choose between God and "the world," between living out of his own resources and the values that the world provides, or opening himself up to the Will of God. To fall back upon the reconstruction of factual data from the life of Jesus is to seek worldly props and proofs for faith.

Bultmann saw demythologizing as an attempt to set free the essential message of the New Testament from what he regarded as the embarrassment of its mythological formulation. For Bultmann the real stumbling block was the acceptance of the cross and the surrender of self-sufficiency. Why make this surrender more difficult for modern man by putting in his way the additional stumbling block of a mythology which he can no longer believe while maintaining his intellectual integrity? What Bultmann seemed unaware of was that his "demythologizing" was really a "re-mythologizing" using the existentialist categories of Martin Heidegger.

Lewis was concerned that the modernist attempt to demythologize the New Testament would mean not only that the Gospel record would be taken less seriously, but also that one would descend to a lower level of reality. As Lewis pointed out in his discussion of myth, when one abstracts meaning from a myth one talks about the myth rather than experiencing it in its fullest depths of meaning and insight. As he writes in Letters to Malcolm, "Did you ever meet, or hear of, anyone who converted from skepticism to a 'liberal' or 'de-mythologized' Christianity? I think that when unbelievers come in at all, they come in a good deal further."[6]

Still, Bultmann and Lewis may have had more in common than either man was aware. Bultmann stressed the kerygma of the early church as having first importance and developed an indifference to the historical reality behind that kerygma. Lewis stressed the mythic nature of Christianity as a validation of the historical reality. However, in his *Narnia Chronicles* Lewis showed that the Christian story has a mythic power that is independent of the historical reality. Thus, both Lewis and Bultmann recognized the *kerygma* and radical obedience to it as the essence of Christianity. Both also rejected the notion of a successful quest for the historical Jesus, and both eschewed psycho-history.

Where Lewis and Bultmann disagreed most clearly was on the nature and power of the Christian myth. Bultmann saw the need to demythologize Christianity to make it accessible to modern man. Lewis saw that by demythologizing Christianity Bultmann removed the numinous element of the Christian message and unconsciously substituted a poorer mythology for a richer one.

One of Lewis's major problems with this demythologized or "naturalistic" Christianity is its denial of the possibilities of the supernatural. As Lewis saw it, "Isn't it possible that many 'liberals' have a highly illiberal motive for banishing the idea of Heaven? They want the gilt-edged security of a religion so contrived that no possible fact could ever refute it. . . . But surely the sort of religion they want would consist of nothing but tautologies."[7]

But one does not have to reject the possibilities of the supernatural while recognizing the ambiguous nature of historical records. Van A. Harvey, in his book *The Historian and the Believer*, recognized that our judgements about the past cannot simply be classified as true or false but must be seen as claiming only a greater or a lesser degree of probability and as always open to revision. Further, stated Harvey, it is impossible to assess the degree of probability of orthodox assertions because in the realm of the supernatural any discussion of possibility and probability flounders.[8]

But, claimed Harvey, one's degree of Christian faith does not depend on one's factual knowledge about the historical Jesus. As Harvey described it: "Faith has to do with one's confidence in God, which is to say, with one's surrender of his attempts to establish his own righteousness and his acceptance of his life and creation as a gift and a responsibility. It is trust and commitment. This awareness, to be sure, may be linked in the minds of some people with certain historical beliefs, but it is by no means clear that it must necessarily be so linked."[9]

Van Harvey concluded that the content of faith can be mediated through a myth as well as through history and saw this contrast in the "historical Jesus" and the "Christ of faith." As Van Harvey summed up his perspective: "If the understanding of man before God implicit. . . in the historical Jesus (when that refers to a certain kind of historical reconstruction) is the same understanding that is given through the kerygma of a dying and rising savior-god, then the decision of faith in both cases is the same: Can the last power be trusted? Is God gracious? Is my life significant in some sense that transcends the world?"[10]

In a like manner, H. Richard Niebuhr has argued that the power of a paradigmatic historical event is precisely the fusion of universality and particularity. Once this principle is grasped, symbol and history are not seen as opposites. As Niebuhr described it: "History may function as myth or as symbol when men use it . . . for understanding their present and future. When we grasp our present, not so much as a product of our past, but more as essentially revealed in that past, then the historical account is necessarily symbolic; it is not merely descriptive of what was once the case."[11]

Given Niebuhr's insight into the uses of history as myth and symbol, perhaps it is in Lewis's view of myth that one finds his most helpful defense of Christianity. Lewis had no difficulty obtaining theological insights of profound importance from the Old Testament, even though he himself freely admitted that portions of the Old Testament were historical while other portions were mythological. It was only when Lewis came to the New Testament that he claimed the material found there was almost totally historical, "myth become fact."

For Lewis the embodiment of myth in historical reality paralleled, and in a sense, duplicated the Incarnation: "It is not an accidental resemblance that what, from the point of view of being, is stated in the form 'God became Man,' should involve, from the point of view of human knowledge, the statement

'Myth became Fact.' The essential meaning of all things came down from the 'heaven' of myth to the 'earth' of history. . . . The humiliation of God and the shrinking or condensation of the myth as it becomes fact are also quite real."[12]

Although Lewis claimed Christianity to be "myth become fact", never in his writings did he provide the necessary basis for this assertion. As we have seen, various historians have disagreed over the historical nature of the Gospel record, some claiming greater or lesser historical validity but all recognizing the problematical nature of the New Testament record itself. While Lewis had pointed out some valid criticisms of certain types of New Testament research, he did not really come to grips with the basic core results of that research or even the textual criticism of the New Testament documents themselves.

As Lewis recognized, finite beings have no absolute knowledge of the Infinite God, only analogies, mythical models, symbols, and abstractions. But it was in the realm of myth that man responded most fully, as a whole person, to the supernatural realm. Perhaps Lewis's concern for the historical nature of the Christian fulfillment of the dying and rising god motif of pagan mythologies was misplaced. Could not the Christian story be the mythical fulfillment of these stories of "pagan christs"? One could state that Christianity is "myth become religious fact," the fact of a New Testament Church guided by a new vision and understanding of reality. Christianity could then be seen as Lewis saw the Old Testament, the "chosen mythology" of God.

For Lewis, the validity of the Christian story resulted in large part from the fact that it made concrete what had previously been only imagined or hinted at in both pagan and Jewish thought. As Lewis saw it: "What is everywhere and always imageless and ineffable, only to be glimpsed in dream and symbol and the acted poetry of ritual becomes small, solid--no bigger than a man who can lie asleep in a rowing boat on the Lake of Galilee."[13]

Lewis accepted the historical reality of the Christian story because for him it was the fulfillment and embodiment of the mythic world of both pagan and

Jewish thought. Lewis declared: "I believe in Christianity as I believe the sun has risen, not only because I see it, but because by it I see everything else."[14] What Lewis failed to recognize is that this "mythic" Incarnation may make irrelevant the historical research into the facts behind the creation of this Christian world view.

Lewis showed in <u>The Narnia Chronicles</u> that the realities of the Gospel can be transposed into a fictional world like Narnia without distorting or detracting from the Christian message. The <u>Narnia Chronicles</u> succeed as religious fantasy because the truth of the "myth" they present is prior to and independent of any historical judgements or findings.

Only in interpreting Christianity as myth does Lewis avoid the problems of the historicity of the Gospels. And in recreating this mythological world view in his <u>Narnia Chronicles</u>, Lewis showed the tremendous power of the Christian story in another context. As Joseph Sobran commented on Lewis's later and more imaginative writings: "They are less ambitious but more satisfying than his apologetic books, because they release his imagination from the burden of trying to satisfy skepticism. Instead they show the power of Christianity, once accepted, to illuminate diverse areas of life. His children's stories prove nothing, but they impart a vision of reality that makes most fiction seem drab and feeble by comparison."[15]

Is this to deny the historicity of much of the Gospel record? No. Scholars and layman may reflect various points of view concerning the historical basis of the New Testament Church, and new discoveries may call for further re-evaluation of the Gospel texts. But, as Lewis himself recognized, most Christians of the first century were converted by the <u>kerygma</u> of the early church rather than by an encounter with the historical Jesus. In other words, it was the "Christ of faith," rather than the "Jesus of history" who formed the basis of the early Christian community, even though the historical Jesus marked the beginnings of that faith.

Lewis might have found the above argument an attempt at having it both ways, an exercise in what he called "liberal" theology. It is not. The

Christian view of the universe is either correct, or it is not. There is either a God who cares for and desires the redemption of man, or there is not. Whether the historical documents of the New Testament Church reflect an accurate portrayal of Jesus's nature and mission can be debated. But the basic "truths" of Christian faith, of a loving and caring God, of a supernatural realm which in some sense intervenes in the world of the everyday, these must be held to be in some sense valid, or Christianity cannot be seen as a useful way of interpreting humanity and the world.

Lewis's life as an apologist for the Christian faith has helped make the Christian world view a reality for modern man. By analyzing the human condition, the sense of longing or <u>Sehnsucht</u> for ultimate fulfillment, and man's consistent affirmation of and appreciation for a moral law, Lewis has shown that the Christian "myth" fulfills many of the basic needs and wants of a mankind Walker Percy has described as "lost in the cosmos." Lewis, by affirming the truth of myth, also affirmed the truth of the Christian faith.

Lewis recognized that all his arguments did not <u>prove</u> the validity of his faith. As he wrote in the last book completed before his death: "And yet. . . after all. I know. It is a venture. We don't <u>know</u> it will be. There is our freedom."[16] But throughout his religious writings, Lewis ultimately affirmed the power of the Christian faith, regardless of his own attempts to defend it. His final comments on his role as apologist are found on the last page of <u>Letters to Malcolm</u>: "Guesses, of course, only guesses. If they are not true, something better will be. For 'we know that we shall be made like Him, for we shall see Him as He is.'"[17]

NOTES: CHAPTER FIVE

¹C. S. Lewis, "Cross-Examination," God in the Dock (Grand Rapids: William B. Erdmans, 1970) ed. Walter Hooper, p.262.

²C. S. Lewis, "Historicism," Christian Reflections, ed. Walter Hooper, (Grand Rapids: William B. Eerdmans, 1970) p. 107.

³Lewis, "Myth Became Fact," God in the Dock, p. 64.

⁴Rudolf Bultmann, Jesus Christ and Mythology (New York: Charles Scribner's Sons, 1958), p. 18.

⁵Bultmann, Jesus Christ and Mythology, p. 18.

⁶C. S. Lewis, Letters to Malcolm: Chiefly on Prayer (New York: Harcourt Brace Jovanovich, 1964), p. 119.

⁷Lewis, Malcolm, p. 121.

⁸Van A. Harvey, The Historian and the Believer: The Morality of Historical Knowledge and Christian Belief (New York: The Macmillan Company, 1966) pp 14-15.

⁹Harvey, p. 280.

¹⁰Harvey, p. 281.

¹¹H. Richard Niebuhr, The Responsible Self (New York: Harper and Row, 1963), p. 156.

¹²C. S. Lewis, "Is Theology Poetry," The Weight of Glory, pp 84-85.

¹³Lewis, Weight of Glory, p. 85.

¹⁴Lewis, Weight of Glory, p. 92.

¹⁵Joseph Sobran, "The Poor Man's Aquinas," National Review, 37, (May 31, 1985), p. 43.

¹⁶Lewis, Letters to Malcolm, pp. 120-121.

[17]Lewis, *Letters to Malcolm*, p. 124.

BIBLIOGRAPHY

Books by C. S. Lewis

Lewis, Clive Staples. The Abolition of Man. New York: Macmillan, 1946.

----------. The Allegory of Love: A Study in Medieval Tradition. London: Oxford University Press paperback, 1958.

----------. The Business of Heaven: Daily Readings from C. S. Lewis, ed. Walter Hooper. New York: Harcourt Brace Jovanovich, 1984.

----------. The Discarded Image: An Introduction to Medieval and Renaissance Literature. London: Cambridge University Press, 1964.

----------. Christian Reflections. ed. Walter Hooper. Grand Rapids: William B. Eerdmans, 1966.

----------. The Dark Tower and Other Stories. ed. Walter Hooper. New York: Harcourt Brace Jovanovich, 1977.

----------. English Literature in the Sixteenth Century Excluding Drama: The Oxford History of English Literature, Vol. III. Oxford: Clarendon Press, 1954.

----------, ed. Essays Presented to Charles Williams. 1947; rpt. Grand Rapids: William B. Eerdmans, 1966.

----------. An Experiment in Criticism. Cambridge: Cambridge University Press, 1961.

----------. The Four Loves. New York: Harcourt Brace and World, 1960.

----------, ed. George MacDonald: An Anthology. New York: Macmillan, 1947.

----------. God in the Dock. ed. Walter Hooper. Grand Rapids: William B. Eerdmans, 1970.

----------. The Great Divorce. 1946; rpt. New York: Macmillan paperback, 1975.

----------. A Grief Observed. New York: Bantam Books, 1976.

----------. The Horse and His Boy. 1954; rpt. New York: Collier Books, 1970.

----------. The Joyful Christian; 127 Readings from C. S. Lewis. ed. Henry William Griffin. New York: Macmillan, 1977.

----------. The Last Battle. 1956; rpt. New York: Collier Books, 1970.

----------. Letters of C. S. Lewis. ed. W. H. Lewis. New York: Harcourt Brace Jovanovich, 1966.

----------. Letters to an American Lady. ed. Clyde Kilby. Grand Rapids: William B. Eerdmans, 1967.

----------. Letters to Children. eds. Lyle W. Dorsett and Majorie Lamp Mead. New York: Macmillan, 1985.

----------. The Lion, the Witch, and the Wardrobe. 1950; rpt. New York: Collier Books, 1970.

----------. Letters to Malcolm: Chiefly on Prayer. New York: Harcourt Brace Jovanovich, 1964.

----------. The Magician's Nephew. 1955; rpt. New York: Collier Books, 1970.

----------. Mere Christianity. New York: Macmillan paperback, 1960.

----------. A Mind Awake: An Anthology of C. S. Lewis. ed. Clyde S. Kilby. Grand Rapids: William B. Eerdmans, 1967.

----------. Miracles: A Preliminary Study with Revision of Chapter III. New York: Macmillan paperback, 1978.

----------. Of Other Worlds: Essays and Stories. ed. Walter Hooper. New York: Harcourt Brace Jovanovich, 1966.

----------. *On Stories: and Other Essays on Literature*. ed. Walter Hooper. New York: Harcourt Brace Jovanovich, 1982.

----------. *Out of the Silent Planet*. 1938; rpt. New York: Macmillan paperback, 1965.

----------. *Perelandra*. 1944; rpt. New York: Macmillan paperback, 1960.

----------. *The Pilgrim's Regress: An Allegorical Apology for Christianity, Reason, and Romanticism*. 2nd ed. 1943; rpt. Grand Rapids: William B. Eerdmans, 1958.

----------. *Poems*. ed. Walter Hooper. New York: Harcourt Brace Jovanovich, 1964.

----------. *A Preface to Paradise Lost*. London: Oxford University Press, 1942.

----------. *Present Concerns: Essays by C. S. Lewis*. ed. Walter Hooper. New York: Harcourt Brace Jovanovich, 1986.

----------. *Prince Caspian: The Return to Narnia*. 1951; rpt. New York: Collier Books, 1970.

----------. *The Problem of Pain*. New York: Macmillan, 1961.

----------. *Reflections on the Psalms*. New York: Harcourt Brace and World, 1958.

----------. *The Screwtape Letters: with Screwtape Proposes a Toast*. New York: Macmillan paperback, 1975.

----------. *Selected Literary Essays*. ed. Walter Hooper. Cambridge: Cambridge University Press, 1969.

----------. *The Silver Chair*. 1953; rpt. New York: Collier Books, 1970.

----------. *Spirits in Bondage: A Cycle of Lyrics*. ed. Walter Hooper. New York: Harcourt Brace Jovanovich, 1984.

----------. *Spenser's Images of Life.* ed. Alastair Fowler. Cambridge: Cambridge University Press, 1967.

----------. *Studies in Medieval and Renaissance Literature.* ed. Walter Hooper. Cambridge: Cambridge University Press, 1966.

----------. *Studies in Words.* 2nd ed. Cambridge: Cambridge University Press, 1967.

----------. *Surprised by Joy: The Shape of My Early Life.* New York: Harcourt Brace and World, 1956.

----------. *That Hideous Strength: A Modern Fairy Tale for Grown-Ups*, 1946; rpt. New York: Macmillan paperback, 1965.

----------. *They Stand Together: The Letters of C. S. Lewis to Arthur Greeves (1914-1963).* ed. Walter Hooper. New York: Macmillan, 1979.

----------. *Till We Have Faces.* 1957; rpt. Grand Rapids: William B.. Eerdmans, 1964.

----------. *The Voyage of the 'Dawn Treader'.* 1952; rpt. New York: Collier Books, 1970.

----------. *The Visionary Christian: 131 Readings from C. S. Lewis.* ed. Chad Walsh. New York: Macmillan, 1981.

----------. *The Weight of Glory And Other Addresses: Revised and Expanded Edition.* ed. Walter Hooper. New York: Macmillan, 1980.

----------. *The World's Last Night: And Other Essays.* New York: Harcourt Brace and World, 1960.

Secondary Sources

Aeschliman, Michael D. *The Restitution of Man: C. S. Lewis and the Case Against Scientism.* Grand Rapids: William B. Eerdmans, 1983.

Anderson, Hugh, ed. *Jesus: Great Lives Observed.* Englewood Cliffs, N. J.: Prentice-Hall, 1967.

Barratt, David. *C. S. Lewis and his World.* Grand Rapids: William B. Eerdmans, 1987.

Bartsch, H. W., ed. *Kerygma and Myth.* New York: Harper and Row, 1961.

Beversluis, John. *C. S. Lewis and the Search for Rational Religion.* Grand Rapids: William B. Eerdmans, 1985.

Bultmann, Rudolf and K. Kundsin, *Form Criticism: Two Essays on New Testament Research.* trans. F. C. Grant. New York: Harper Torchbooks, 1962.

Bultmann, Rudolf. *History of the Synoptic Tradition.* trans. John Marsh. New York: Harper and Row, 1963.

----------. *Jesus Christ and Mythology.* New York: Charles Scribner's Sons, 1958.

----------. *Jesus and the Word.* trans. Louise Pettibone Smith and Erminie Huntress Lantero. New York: Charles Scribner's Sons, 1934.

----------. *The Presence of Eternity.* New York: Harper and Row, 1957.

----------. *Primitive Christianity in its Contemporary Setting.* New York: Meridian, 1956.

----------. *Theology of the New Testament.* Vol. I. trans. Kendrick Grobel. London: S. C. M. Press, 1952.

Carnell, Corbin S. *Bright Shadow of Reality: C. S. Lewis and the Feeling Intellect.* Grand Rapids: William B. Eerdmans, 1974.

Carpenter, Humphrey. *The Inklings: C. S. Lewis, J. R. R. Tolkien, Charles Williams and their Friends*. Boston: Houghton Mifflin, 1978.

Christensen, Michael. *C. S. Lewis on Scripture: His Thoughts on the Nature of Biblical Inspiration, the Role of Revelation and the Question of Inerrancy*. Waco, Texas: Word Books, 1979.

Christopher, Joe R., and Joan K. Ostling, *C. S. Lewis: An Annotated Checklist of Writings About Him and His Works*. Kent, Ohio: Kent State University Press, 1974.

Como, James T., ed. *C. S. Lewis at the Breakfast Table: And Other Reminiscences*. New York: Macmillan, 1979.

Dodd, C. H. *The Interpretation of the Fourth Gospel*. Cambridge: Cambridge University Press, 1953.

Dorsett, Lyle W. *And God Came In: The Extraordinary Story of Joy Davidman*. New York: Ballantine Books, 1983.

Gibb, Jocelyn, Ed. *Light on C. S. Lewis*. New York: Harcourt Brace Jovanovich, 1965.

Green, Roger Lancelyn and Walter Hooper. *C. S. Lewis: A Biography*. New York: Harcourt Brace Jovanovich, 1974.

Griffin, William. *C. S. Lewis: A Dramatic Life*. San Francisco: Harper and Row, 1986.

Hannay, Margaret Patterson. *C. S. Lewis*. New York: Frederick Ungar Pub. Co., 1981.

Harnack, Adolf von. *What is Christianity?*. New York: Harper and Row, 1957.

Hart, Dabney Adams. *Through the Open Door: A New Look at C. S. Lewis*. University Alabama: University of Alabama Press, 1984.

Harvey, Van A. *The Historian and the Believer: The Morality of Historical Knowledge and Christian Belief*. New York: The Macmillan Company, 1966.

Holmer, Paul L. C. S. Lewis: The Shape of His Faith and Thought. New York: Harper and Row, 1976.

Hooper, Walter. Past Watchful Dragons: The Narnian Chronicles of C. S. Lewis. New York: Collier Books, 1979.

----------. Through Joy and Beyond: A Pictorial Biography of C. S. Lewis. New York: The Macmillian Co., 1982.

Karkainen, Paul A. Narnia Explored. Old Tappan N. J.: Fleming H. Revell Co., 1979.

Kee, Howard Clark. Jesus in History: An Approach to the Study of the Gospels. 2nd ed. New York: Harcourt Brace Jovanovich, 1977.

Keefe, Carolyn, ed. C. S. Lewis: Speaker and Teacher. Grand Rapids: Zondervan, 1971.

Kilby, Clyde S. The Christian World of C. S. Lewis. Grand Rapids: William B. Eerdmans, 1964.

----------. Images of Salvation in the Fiction of C. S. Lewis. Wheaton, Il.: Harold Shaw Publishers, 1978.

Kreeft, Peter. C. S. Lewis: A Critical Essay. Grand Rapids: William B. Eerdmans, 1969.

Lewis, Warren H. Brothers and Friends: The Diaries of Major Warren Hamilton Lewis. eds. Clyde S. Kilby and Marjorie Lamp Mead. San Francisco: Harper and Row, 1982.

Lindskoog, Kathryn. C. S. Lewis: Mere Christian. Glendale, Cal.: Gospel Light Publications, 1973.

----------. The Lion of Judah in Never-Never Land: The Theology of C. S. Lewis Expressed in His Fantasies for Children. Grand Rapids: William B. Eerdmans, 1973.

Locke, John. The Reasonableness of Christianity. ed. I. T. Ramsey. Stanford, 1958.

Marty, Martin E. and Dean G. Peerman, eds. A

Meilaender, Gilbert. *The Taste for the Other: The Social and Ethical Thought of C. S. Lewis.* Grand Rapids: William B. Eerdmans, 1978.

Moynihan, Martin. *The Latin Letters of C. S. Lewis* Westchester Il.: Crossway Books, 1987.

Niebuhr, Richard H. *The Responsible Self.* New York: Harper and Row, 1963.

Payne, Leanne. *Real Presence: The Holy Spirit in the Works of C. S. Lewis.* Westchester Il.: Cornerstone Books, 1979.

Perrin, Norman. *What is Redaction Criticism?.* Philadelphia: Fortress Press, 1969.

Petersen, William J. *C. S. Lewis Had a Wife* Wheaton Il.: Tyndale House Publishers, 1985.

Purtill, Richard L. *C. S. Lewis's Case for the Christian Faith.* San Francisco: Harper and Row, 1981.

Ryken, Leland. *The Literature of the Bible.* Grand Rapids: Zondervan, 1974.

Schakel, Peter J., ed. *The Longing for a Form: Essays on the Fiction of C. S. Lewis.* Grand Rapids: Baker Book House, 1979.

----------. *Reading with the Heart: The Way into Narnia.* Grand Rapids: William B. Eerdmans, 1979.

----------. *Reason and Imagination in C. S. Lewis: A Study of Till We Have Faces.* Grand Rapids: William B. Eerdmans, 1984.

Schweitzer, Albert. *The Quest of the Historical Jesus.* Introd. James M. Robinson. New York: Macmillan, 1961.

Smith, Robert Houston. *Patches of Godlight: The Pattern of Thought of C. S. Lewis.* Athens: University of Georgia Press, 1981.

Tillich, Paul. *Dynamics of Faith*. New York: Harper and Row, Torchbook edition, 1958.

Vanauken, Sheldon. *A Severe Mercy*. New York: Harper and Row, Bantam ed., 1979.

Walsh, Chad. *C. S. Lewis: Apostle to the Skeptics*. New York: Macmillan, 1949.

----------. *The Literary Legacy of C. S. Lewis*. New York: Harcourt Brace Jovanovich, 1979.

White, William Luther. *The Image of Man in C. S. Lewis*. Nashville: Abingdon Press, 1969.

Willis, John Randolph, S. J. *Pleasures Forevermore: The Theology of C. S. Lewis*. Chicago: Loyola University Press, 1983.

INDEX

Acts of the Apostles, 64-65, 77
Adonis, 34, 70
Aeneid, 107
Aeschylus, 29
Agape and Eros, 15
Alexander the Great, 57
Alexander, Samuel 30-31
All Hallows Eve, 19
Anscombe, Elizabeth, 6, 81, 82
Anthroposophy, 20
Apocrapha, 46
Aquinas, Thomas (saint), 12
Archetypes, 15, 109
Ariel, 90
Aristotle, 10, 12
Aslan, 7, 87, 95, 97ff.
   Parallels to Christ, 106ff.
Attila the Hun, 57
Auden, W. H., 1
Augustine (saint), 10

Bacchus, 34
Balder, 34, 39, 40, 42
Barfield, Owen, 19, 20, 29, 32, 33
Barth, Karl, 11, 14
Berdyaev, Nicolas, 13
Berger, Peter, 31
Berkeley, George, 31
Bevan, Edwyn, 15
Bible, 18, 43, 44, 46
   As parallel to Narnia Chronicles, 110-111
Boswell, James, 47, 58, 94
Bradley, F. H., 31
Bright Shadow of Reality, 1
British Broadcasting Company, 5
Buber, Martin, 14-15
Buddhism, Zen, 39
Bultmann, Rudolf, 13, 57-58, 60, 66-67, 68, 73ff., 122-123, 124
Bunyan, John, 36

Calvin, John, 43
Carnell, Corbin Scott, 1, 12, 77, 78
Carpenter, Humphrey, 14, 22n., 35
Chalcedon, Council of, 88
Chesterton, G. K., 15, 28, 29, 31
Christian Herald, 96
Christianity as Old As Creation, 72
Coghill, Nevill, 29, 34
Cox, Harvey, 13
Cupid, 2, 8

Daniel, The Book of, 60
Dante, 10, 107
David, (King), 43
Deborah, 92
Deism, 12
Demeter, 42
Demythologize, 16, 113, 123
Descartes, Rene, 12
Docetism, 88, 89
Dodd, C. H., 79
Dynamics of Faith, 112
Dyson, "Hugo", 19, 33

Enlightenment, ix, 47, 56
Ethics, (Aristotle's), 11
Euhemerus, ix
Euripides, 30
Everlasting Man, 15, 31

Faire Queene, 3
Falstaff, 58
Frazier, James, 18, 32
Form criticism, 73ff., 80
Fundamentalist, 43, 93

Gautama (the Buddha), 91
Genesis, 44
Gibbon, Edward, 14, 29
Gilson, Etienne, 1, 12
Golden Bough, 18
God, 7, 12, 20, 28, 31-32, 33,
   34, 35, 36-37, 40, 41ff., 45,
   46, 70, 125
   Incarnation of, 88ff.
   Kingdom of, 63ff.
Gospels, 32, 33, 34, 47, 57,
   58, 59, 60, 62, 63, 66, 69,
   99, 122, 127
   Historical validity of,
      77ff.
   Literary qualities of, 90ff.
Graham, Fred, 95
Green, Roger Lancelyn, 2, 22n.
Greeves, Arthur, 16, 27, 33,
   34, 35, 37, 89
Gresham, Joy Davidman, 8
Griffin, William, 22n.

Hanney, Margaret Patterson, ix
Harnack, Adolf, 59, 61, 63, 65
Hart, Dabney Adams, 96, 111, 112
Hartshorne, Charles, 1, 12
Harvey, Van A., 124-125
Hebrews, 27, 43, 45, 92, 94
Hegel, G. W. F., 31
Heidegger, Martin, 122-123
Heracles, 27
Herbert, George, 10
Hesperides, 42
Hinduism, 68
Historian and the Believer, 124
Historical Jesus Movement, 61ff.
History of Synoptic Traditon, 73
Hippolytus, 30
Hitler, Adolph, 11
Holmer, Paul, 1
Holtzmann, Heinrich, 72
Homer, 107
Honest to God, 14
Hooker, Richard, 10
Hooper, Walter, 22n., 33, 97,
   99, 103, 105
Hosea, 106

Humanity of God, 14
Huttar, Charles, 98, 107, 110

I and Thou, 14-15
Idea of the Holy, 15
Inferno, 107
Imitation of Christ, 10
Industrial Revolution, 7
Inklings, 19-20
Islam, 69
Israel, 42, 62, 92

Jadis, see White Witch
Jenkins, A. K. Hamilton, 33
Jeremiah, 91
Jerome (saint), 43
Jesus Christ, 6, 15, 16, 27,
   28, 33, 34, 35, 42, 47-48
   And the Gospels, 71ff.
   And Miracles, 67ff.
   As Maledil, 96-97
   Divinity of, 56ff.
   Incarnation of, 66, 70,
      87ff., 97
   In Gethsemane, 77, 90
   Kingdom of God, views of,
      63ff.
   Teachings of, 45-46, 91ff.
Jews, 46, 56, 59, 64, 126
Job, 4, 43
John, Gospel According to, 33,
   64, 79-80, 94, 106
Joseph, (saint), 69
Johnson, Samuel, 29, 49, 58, 94
Jonah, 44, 79
Jung, Carl, 15-16

Kant, Immanuel, 13
Kafka, Franz, 17
Karkainen, Paul, 99
Kerygma, 57, 62, 123-124, 125,
   127
Kierkegaard, Soren, 13-14
Kilby, Clyde, 44
Kirke, Digory, 100, 101, 105
Kirkpatrick, W. T., 17-18

142

Law, William, 10
Lazarus, 90
Lewis, C. S.,
　As atheist, 18, 27-28
　At Cambridge, 7
　At Oxford, 7, 28, 29
　Childhood, 2-3
　Conversion of, 7, 28ff.
　Marriage, 8-9
　Military Service, 28
　Old Western Man, 7-8
　Views of:
　　Gospels, 71ff.
　　Incarnation, 66, 87ff.
　　Jesus's Divinity, 57ff.
　　Jesus's teachings, 91ff.
　　Kingdom of God, 63ff.
　　Miraculous, 68ff.
　　Myth, ix, 35ff., 112, 125ff.
　　Sehnsucht, 7, 30-31, 39, 128
　　Space travel, 96
　Works,
　　Abolition of Man, 5, 98
　　Allegory of love, 1, 3, 4, 11
　　Beyond Personality, 5
　　Broadcast Talks, 5
　　Christian Behavior, 5
　　Christian Reflections, 10
　　Discarded Image, 10, 111
　　Dymer, 3
　　English Literature in the Sixteenth Century, 6
　　Experiment in Criticism, 9, 38-39, 113
　　Four Loves, 8
　　God in the Dock, 10
　　Great Divorce, 5, 19, 98
　　Grief Observed, 4, 9
　　Horse and His Boy, 6, 104
　　Last Battle, 2, 6, 105, 106, 108, 110, 112
　　Letters to Malcolm, 9, 14-15, 109, 113, 123, 128
　　Lion, Witch, and the Wardrobe, 6, 101ff.

Lewis, C. S., (continued)
　Works,
　　Magician's Nephew, 6, 100ff., 105
　　Mere Christianity, 5, 91, 95, 98
　　Miracles, 5, 6, 8, 42, 55, 68, 78, 81, 95
　　Narnia Chronicles, 1, 6, 82, 87, 95, 97ff., 110, 127-128
　　On Stories, 10
　　Out of the Silent Planet, 1, 4, 95
　　Perelandra, 5, 15, 19, 96, 97-98
　　Personal Heresy, 4
　　Pilgrim's Regress, 3, 20, 36, 41, 42
　　Preface to Paradise Lost, 1, 4, 98
　　Prince Caspian, 6, 107
　　Present Concerns, 10
　　Problem of Pain, 4, 90, 98
　　Reflections on the Psalms, 6, 8, 43
　　Rehabilitations, 4
　　Screwtape Letters, 4-5, 19, 61-62, 98
　　Selected Literary Essays, 10
　　Silver Chair, 6, 95, 104
　　Spenser's Images of Life, 10
　　Spirits in Bondage, 3
　　Studies in Medieval and Renaissance Literature, 10
　　Studies in Words, 9
　　Surprised by Joy, 7, 16, 18-19, 28, 34
　　That Hideous Strength, 1, 5, 18, 98
　　Till We Have Faces, 2, 8
　　Transpositional, 6
　　Voyage of the "Dawn Treader", 6, 106, 107
　　World's Last Night, 9

Lewis, Joy Davidman (Gresham), 8–9
Lewis, Warren, 2, 34
Liberation Theology, 61
Lock, Walter, 79
Locke, John, 72
Lord of the Rings, 19, 21, 76
Luke, Gospel According to, 63, 66, 71, 73, 77
Luther, Martin, 72

MacDonald, George, 16–17, 28, 29
Magdalen College, 30
Magnificat, 92
Malacandra (Mars), 95, 98
Maledil, 95–96, 97
Man Born to be King, 19
Marcel, Gabriel, 14
Marcus Aurelius, 91
Mark, Gospel According to, 56–57, 61, 63, 65–66, 73, 74, 75, 77, 78
Maritain, Jacques, 13
Marxism, 61, 62
Mary, Mother of Jesus, 69, 92
Matthew, Fr. Gervase, 19
Matthew, Gospel According to, 63, 73, 77
Meilander, Gilbert, 1, 101, 108
"Messianic secret", 57
Messisgeheimnis in the den Evangelien (Messianic Secret in the Gospels), 57
Mill, John Stuart, 29
Milton, John, 4, 10, 29
Mohammedanism, see Islam
Moses, 43
Myth, 2, 8, 14, 15–16, 17, 20, 29, 35–36, 67, 78, 107, 122–123
  Lewis's views of, 35ff., 112, 125ff.
  Narnia Chronicle as, 99–100
  "Myth become fact", ix, 17, 34, 39–40, 43, 47, 55, 62, 71, 73, 87, 113, 121, 125ff.

New Testament, 5, 45, 47–48, 55, 58, 64, 65, 68, 70, 72, 74, 76–77, 82, 111, 112, 122, 125, 126–127
Niebuhr, H. Richard, 125
Nygren, Anders, 15

Odin, 27
Odyssey, 107
Old Testament, 43ff. 77–78, 125
Orpheus, 42, 70
Osiris, 40, 70
Otto, Rudolf, 15

Pantheism, 12
Paradise Lost, 79
Pascal, Blaise, 31
Paul of Tarsus (saint), 57, 123
Percy, Walker, 128
Perelandra (Venus), 96–97, 98
Persephone, 42
Peter (saint), 63, 75, 76
Pevensie children,
  Edmund, 101–102, 106
  Lucy, 101, 102, 103, 106, 107
  Peter, 101
  Susan, 101, 102, 103
Phantastes, 17, 28,
Pole Jill, 104–105, 107
Psyche, 2, 8
Psalms, 6, 146

Quelle, 72
Quest of the Historical Jesus, 63–64

Reasonableness of Christianity, 72
Redaction criticism, 74–75
Reimarus, Hermann Samuel, 56
Renaissance, 6, 7, 10
Revelation to John, 106
Robinson, John A. T., 13, 14

Roman Catholicism, 31, 72, 93
Roosevelt, Franklin, 11

Sayers, Dorothy, 19
Schakel, Peter, 81-82, 99-100, 103, 109
Shakespeare, William, 65
Schopenhauer, Arthur, 18
Scrubb, Eustace, 104, 107, 108
Schweitzer, Albert, 48, 63-64, 75
Serious Call, 10
Sein und Zeit (Being and Time), 122
Shaw, George Bernard, 29
Sitz im Leben, 76
Smith, Robert Huston, 96, 97, 98
Sobran, Joseph, 127
Socrates, 47, 58, 91, 94
Son of Man, 60-61, 64, 80
Space, Time, and Deity, 30
Spenser, Edmund, 3, 10, 29
Spinoza, Baruch, 13
Stoics, 90, 96
Summa Theologica, 11
Symbolism and Belief, 15
Synoptic Gospels: Their Origin and Historical Character, 72
Synoptic problem, 76-77, 80

Tacitus, 79
Tash, 108-109
Tegner's Drapa, 39
Teilhard de Chardin, Pierre, 14
Tertullos, 77
Theology of the New Testament, 74
Thomas a Kempis, 10
Thucydides, 79
Thulcandra (earth), 96
Tillich, Paul, 14, 112-113
Tillyard, E. M. W., 4
Tindal, Matthew, 72
Tixier, Elaine, 110-111
Toby, Uncle, 50

Tolkien, J. R. R., 19, 20-21, 30, 33, 36-37, 76, 80, 99
Traherne, Thomas, 10

Virgil, 29, 107
Voltaire, 29

Walsh, Chad, 2, 3, 9, 22n., 69, 78, 106-107, 109
Wells, H. G., 1, 11, 29
What is Christianity?, 59
White, William, 14
White Witch, 101ff.
Whitehead, Alfred North, 13
William of Orange, 57
Williams, Charles, 4, 19-20, 81
Wormwood, 5, 61
Wrede, Wilhelm, 56-57

Zarathustra, 91
Zeitgeist, (spirit of age), 10, 67

ABOUT THE AUTHOR

Mark Edwards Freshwater is currently Division Director of Social Sciences at Snead State Junior College in Boaz, Alabama. He received his Ph. D. in Humanities from Florida State University in 1985.